COPING WITH

Stress

Gwen K. Packard

THE ROSEN PUBLISHING GROUP INC./NEW YORK

Dedicated, with love, to Patricia Elsa Chang, M.D.

Published in 1997 by The Rosen Publishing Group, Inc.
29 East 21st Street, New York, NY 10010

First Edition

Cover photo by Olga Vega

Library of Congress Cataloging-in-Publication Data

Packard, Gwen K.
    Coping with stress / Gwen K. Packard.—1st ed.
        p.   cm.—(Coping)
    Includes bibliographical references and index.
    Summary: A discussion of why teenagers may face stress and what they can do about it, suggesting techniques for dealing with situations such as school difficulties, relationships, and natural disasters.
    ISBN 0-8239-2081-X
    1. Stress in adolescence—Juvenile literature. 2. Stress management for teenagers—Juvenile literature. [Stress (Psychology)] I. Title. II. Series.
BF724.3.S86P33 1997
155.9'042—dc21   96-52137
                                                                                                        CIP
                                                                                                         AC

Manufactured in the United States of America

Acknowledgments

Many thanks to the following people who were generous with their time and knowledge: Ginny Anderson and June Penner, LINKS Youth Health Services; Craig Delamore, WBBM Newsradio, Chicago; Jeanne Felcan, American Red Cross, Mid-America Chapter; Jim Gorski, LCSW; Jane Gaitskill, MSW; Mike Hoffman, social worker, Naperville, Illinois, Police Department; Pamela Holtzman, Cancer Wellness Center; Samuel Huff, high school guidance counselor; Myrna Lopez, Big Brothers and Big Sisters of Metropolitan Chicago; Nancy Love, Charter Hospital; Greg Newman, M.S.; Dana Vance and her eighth-grade class; Charla Waxman, Linden Oaks Hospital.

A special thank-you to Don Packard for information, inspiration, and patience.

I also want to thank the many teens who shared their experiences and opinions with me. Their names have been changed to protect their privacy.

ABOUT THE AUTHOR ◇

G wen K. Packard has a Bachelor of Science in Education from Northwestern University and a Master of Arts in Library Science from Rosary College. She is a member of the American Library Association, Society of Children's Book Writers and Illustrators, Children's Reading Round Table of Chicago, and Off Campus Writers Workshop.

As a freelance writer, Ms. Packard is interested in parenting issues, education, and health care. She is the author of two other books for young adults, *Coping in an Interfaith Family*, and *Coping When a Parent Goes Back to Work*, both published by The Rosen Publishing Group.

Contents

WHAT IS STRESS?

Identifying Stress

Tanika stares out of her bedroom window. It is a beautiful autumn day. The sun is shining, and the multicolored trees sway in the cool breeze. Still, Tanika feels sad and lonely. She has a headache almost all the time and is having trouble sleeping. She wonders why she feels this way.

Tanika used to love autumn. She often went bike riding with her friends, but that was before she and her family moved.

For her dad to be closer to his new job, Tanika, her parents, and brothers moved to a different city three weeks ago. Tanika is attending a new high school, where she is a senior.

The first few days of school were fun, meeting new classmates and teachers. But soon it seemed as if everyone was going his or her own way. Tanika feels isolated, with no friends.

Things had been different for Tanika at her other school. There, she had many friends. She was in the choir and on the student council. She was on the committee that planned the high school's arts weekend, a very important event that gave her the chance to meet local celebrities. She got good grades and still had time for all her activities.

Now Tanika feels that she has to start all over again, making new friends and getting involved with activities. She is also worried about her grades. Her parents can hardly afford to send her to college next year. They have told her that if she gets any grades lower than a B this year, she will probably have to live at home and go to work because she won't get a scholarship. She tries to study as much as possible. Lately, Tanika has added a backache to her other complaints.

RESPONSE TO CHANGE

Tanika is experiencing many major changes in her life. She is facing problems she feels she can't handle. This is causing **stress**, and Tanika's response to that stress is appearing in the form of aches, pains, sadness, and depression.

Stress is often a response to life changes and the need to adjust to those changes. Change may be positive, such as going on vacation or getting a new job, or it may be negative, such as the illness of a parent. Any type of change or disruption in your life—whether it's mental, emotional, or physical—can cause stress. This is especially true if these changes seem to be out of your control.

Stress can make you feel frightened, angry, or even sick. If you feel your problems are too much for you to cope with, if you feel unable to manage your daily life and unable to enjoy it, you are under stress.

You might also be under stress if you have one or several of the many symptoms caused by stress, including:

headaches, backaches, stomachaches, dizziness, rapid heartbeat, depression, anger, anxiety, forgetfulness, or the inability to make decisions. Excessive smoking, drinking, or drug use may also be caused by stress.

As a teenager, you are encountering many changes in your life. You are developing physically, which can be exciting, frightening, and annoying all at the same time. Your mental and emotional outlook is changing as you take on new responsibilities and strive for independence. Your relationships with your friends, family, and the outside world are changing too.

The physical changes that you and all teenagers experience can be as stressful on the emotions as they are on the body. You are probably very much aware of your self-image, and you may not feel emotionally ready for the physical changes that are taking place. You are trying to discover who you are and where you belong in the world. You want to be accepted by your friends.

Although many of the changes in your life are positive, they are all coming at once. You may be graduating from high school and going to work or to college, moving to a new town or city, or starting a new relationship with a girlfriend or boyfriend. Or perhaps your friends are dating and you are feeling stress because you are not. These are all changes that require new thinking, learning, and adapting. All that can create stress.

In addition to facing the many changes that all teens have experienced in the past, today's teens are also exposed to other problems and situations, such as gang violence, drugs and AIDS.

Even more, you are probably faced with events that you have never encountered before. You have no experience to fall back on. And you may be reluctant to discuss your feelings of stress with those people who do have more experience: your parents, teachers, or other adults. Some teens, like Tanika, don't even realize that they are under stress. They just know that something is wrong.

SYMPTOMS OF STRESS

Before you can cope with stress, you need to recognize its symptoms.

"I know I'm getting stressed when I start to yell at everyone," says thirteen-year-old James."If one more person asks me to do one more thing, I feel I'm going to lose it."

"When I have a lot of stress, I get real depressed. I just want everyone to leave me alone," responds James's friend Ramon. "That's not easy when you have three younger sisters."

"I feel like throwing things," says Steve. "One time I did throw my mom's best sewing scissors on the floor and broke them. I can tell you, I had more stress than ever after that. Now I just throw wads of paper in my room."

"Until my junior year in high school, I was getting pretty good grades, and I never had any problems taking tests," says Nancy, seventeen. "Then I started thinking seriously about what college I would attend, and my parents began to put pressure on me to get better grades. I tried to study harder; I gave up after-school sports. Then, the week before any test, I couldn't eat and I couldn't sleep. The morning of a test, I would break out in hives. They looked like huge mosquito bites all over my arms and legs. It was embarrassing. That just added to my problems.

"My parents finally recognized that stress was causing my problems. We sat down and discussed it and tried to work out a plan to help me with my school work without adding so much pressure and stress."

You may think of stress as only an emotional or psychological reaction, that it's "all in your mind." But stress is a lot more than mental activity. When you are under stress, both your mind and body are affected. In fact, stress can affect all aspects of the mind and body: physical, mental, emotional, and spiritual.

Physical and Nonphysical Responses to Stress

Early in human history, the body's response to a stressful situation was important for survival. For example, if a person encountered a wild animal, his choice of response was simple: he could use his weapons to try to kill the animal or use his legs to escape. Experts call this the "fight-or-flight" response. In today's world, the fight-or-flight response can still be useful. It can help us to escape a fire or survive a disaster.

To prepare the body for a fight-or-flight response, the adrenal glands release hormones into the body, increasing the heart rate, breathing rate, and blood pressure. Muscles tense, the digestive system slows down, and eyesight is sharpened. The mind becomes more alert and ready to respond.

Mario experienced the fight-or-flight response on the day he encountered three members of a rival gang, the same ones who had shot Mario's best friend the week before. "If I had been with friends, or if I had had a better weapon with me, I would have stayed to fight, but I just took off. I never ran that fast before in my life. When I got home, I was a wreck. My heart was pounding, my muscles were all tightened up, and I was sick to my stomach. I thought I was having a heart attack."

When you are faced with a stressful situation, called a **stressor**, your body prepares for a fight-or-flight response, with the same physical changes. However, in today's world, that response is not always so simple or appropriate. Fight-or-flight may be useful in times of emergency, but it can be useless or even harmful to the body when reacting to the stresses of everyday life.

For instance, if your parents tell you that they are getting a divorce, a fight-or-flight response is not going to solve the problem or help you deal with the stress. However, your body may still show the same physical symptoms: increased heartbeat and breathing rate, sweaty palms, and tense muscles. Your body reacts much the same way, no matter what the source of the stress is.

When the stressful problem is solved, your body can recover and restore the energy needed for the next response. In the hectic pace of your life, however, you often don't give your body enough time to recover and rest before you face the next stressor. If the source of stress is an ongoing situation, you may feel continual tension, such as an upset stomach or sleeplessness.

Stress can be very powerful. It can deprive you of your sense of control and security and weaken your ability to cope with daily problems. Teenagers are not exempt from the physical symptoms of stress. When you are under stress, the systems of your body, including the immune system, do not function as efficiently as usual. Because stress reduces your body's resistance to disease, it can make you more susceptible to illness and more vulnerable to infection. Stress can lead to symptoms such as migraine headaches, stomachaches, diarrhea, nausea, ulcers, back pain, skin disorders, dizziness, frequent colds, and even tooth decay. It can also cause high blood pressure, which may increase your risk of future heart disease.

Under stress you may also experience muscle tension, rapid heartbeat, intestinal problems, insomnia, or fatigue. If not treated, stress may cause much more serious symptoms, including eating disorders, such as anorexia nervosa and bulimia; panic attacks; phobias; compulsive disorders like extreme cleanliness; violent behavior; depression; or suicide.

Mentally or emotionally, you may experience the inability to concentrate; memory loss; flashes of anger; changes in eating and sleeping patterns; increased use of alcohol, tobacco, and other substances; and prolonged feelings of depression, anxiety, or helplessness. You may cry a lot or get angry for no logical reason. Under stress, you don't think as clearly as usual, so you are more at risk of having an accident or injury while performing activities such as driving or using machinery.

Just as pain is an indication that something is wrong with your body, stress is an indication that some changes need to be made in your life. You need to be aware of stress.

When you don't pay attention to stress or don't cope with it and reduce it, it can have a strong negative effect on your life. Many emotional problems result from stress, such as low self-esteem and difficulty enjoying positive things in your life. You may lose interest in school and stop paying attention in class, allowing your grades to go down; you may withdraw from participation in extracurricular activities and stop hanging out with your friends. You may show extremely good behavior, or antisocial behavior that can't be tolerated in school, such as fighting or taking drugs. If you feel too much pressure to succeed, you may look for ways to fail in order to relieve that pressure.

A high school counselor has observed that some teens, when under stress, lose interest in their appearance.

Many who are usually neat and physically fit suddenly start to dress in a sloppy manner and exhibit poor hygiene.

The physical and emotional symptoms of stress are often the same, no matter what the source of stress. "It's funny, but I actually feel the same stress before a big test as I do before a big game," says sixteen-year-old Connor. "I feel the same before a presentation in history class. My heartbeat and breathing start to race, my palms get sweaty, and my mouth gets dry. Sometimes just thinking about it, I get almost as much stress as I get from the actual event."

Connor's physical reaction to stress is normal and predictable. The physical response is basically the same no matter what the cause. Your mental or emotional reactions to stress are less predictable because they are based on personal factors such as your lifestyle, attitude, emotions, and viewpoint.

When you are under stress, you may feel that things are out of your control, or are hopeless. You may have feelings of anxiety, panic, or frustration. You may feel depressed, guilty, self-conscious, or restless. Your ability to make decisions may be reduced, and you may make more mistakes. You may become angry or impatient for no apparent reason. Under stress, you may overeat or lose your appetite, or turn to alcohol, tobacco, or drugs.

For some teens, stress may even lead to violent or extreme behavior such as vandalism, murder, suicide, or running away. Other teens may withdraw and have low energy and a lack of enthusiasm or hope. Any attention-getting behavior may indicate that a person really does need attention.

The death of a friend or close relative, such as a parent or sibling, adds the symptoms of grief to the list of stress symptoms. You may feel physical pain, and you may want to die, too. Again, in this situation, you have lowered immunity and are more susceptible to disease.

You may experience sudden memory loss and not be able to do simple tasks. You may feel as if you have no strength or energy, feel numb, sad, depressed, or have feelings of guilt.

Following a natural or human-made disaster—such as a flood, hurricane, earthquake, or fire—you may suffer even more symptoms than you would from other sources of stress. You might experience some symptoms before the disaster, as well as after, if there is a warning of impending danger. These additional symptoms caused by disaster include anxiety, fear, flashbacks, nightmares, a lack of emotions, avoidance of responsibility, and the inability to concentrate at work. You may feel dazed, startle easily, or withdraw from friends, family, or the professionals who want to help you.

"After the hurricane hit our town, I couldn't sleep at all," says fourteen-year-old Gill. "I would just think about it all the time. I couldn't do my schoolwork. My boss gave me some time off from work because I was making too many mistakes. I'm glad he didn't fire me. That would only have added to the stress I already had."

Stress can affect you spiritually, too. The spiritual symptoms of stress are different for everyone because each person has his or her own idea of spirituality. Under stress, you may feel isolated from the higher power you usually look to for comfort. You may believe that you must carry all the weight of your stress on your own shoulders. These feelings can add to the stress you are already experiencing.

WHO GETS STRESS?

Paula, seventeen, knows firsthand how differently two people can respond to the same situation. "Last week my friends Carmella and Mimi were in a senior recital. Carmella plays the piano, and Mimi plays the violin. For weeks before the recital, that was all Carmella could talk about. She was frantic. She couldn't sleep; she couldn't eat; she had a constant headache. She complained that her back hurt. She was making mistakes in chemistry, which can get you into trouble.

"On the other hand, Mimi never talked about the recital. She just followed her regular routine and even did a complicated experiment in chemistry that she presented to the whole class. I almost wondered if Mimi had forgotten about the recital; but when I asked her, she just said, 'I'll be ready.'

"Well, Mimi was ready. She played beautifully. Carmella did a great job, too. She's very talented. It's just interesting to me how stressed Carmella was about the recital, and how unstressed Mimi was."

Everyone experiences stress sometimes, but each person may react differently to the same stressors. If you know someone who never seems to be under stress, it may be because, in his or her opinion, a particular situation is not as stressful as you think it is. Some people are more tolerant or resistant to stress. How each individual responds to stress—and whether she even considers a situation stressful—is determined by her own personal characteristics.

The physical response to stress—such as the release of hormones, increased heartrate, and muscle tension—is generally the same for everyone. However, the psychological reaction is not the same. It is controlled by many factors, including someone's personality, viewpoint, emotions, and experience. People can learn to be more stress-resistant.

Different people react differently to the same stressors, depending on personality and coping style. People who are always angry are more likely to be affected by stress and develop stress-related illnesses. Optimistic people cope with stress better than those who have a pessimistic outlook on life. Psychologists classify some people as type A personalities. These people are always under stress. They are competitive and ambitious, but at the same time, they have low self-esteem. They need to prove themselves by trying to accomplish more and more.

An assignment deadline can cause stress for one person and be a challenge and motivation for another. Some people view stressors as challenges rather than obstacles. They have a positive attitude. They are able to work out satisfactory alternatives to problems. These people feel that they are in control of events. Stress is a very individual circumstance. What is stressful for one person is not for another, depending on the situation.

Some people can find good even in a situation they don't like, such as a job. Not only do different people show different reactions to the same stressors, but also the same person may react differently to the same stressor on a different day. If you have ever had a "bad day," when everything seems to go wrong, you may notice that some of the things causing you stress on that day did not bother you in the past. How you view a stressor has an effect on your ability to cope. You can't always change a stressor or get rid of it, but you can change your perception of the stressor and your reaction to it.

WHY COPE WITH STRESS?

Everyone experiences stress. No one's life can be completely free of stress, so it is important to learn how to cope with it.

- **Coping with stress can reduce or eliminate the physical and emotional symptoms associated with stress.** Stress is more than just an emotional annoyance; it also affects your body. If you do not reduce or eliminate stressors, you may encounter serious physical problems. If a stressor is removed or reduced, your body can resist further damage and begin to repair whatever damage has already occurred. If the stressor is not eliminated and continues, your body may develop physical problems, such as migraine headaches, heart irregularity, and stomach disorders.

  If you have physical problems that are caused by stress, you may spend a lot of time and money trying to treat the symptoms of these problems. Coping with the stress directly may eliminate many symptoms.

  Besides physical problems, not coping with stress can also cause a decline in school or job performance and an increase in personal conflicts.

- **Coping with stress can prevent the development of more serious symptoms of stress.** If you are under constant stress, your body's natural defenses are weakened and you are at increased risk for infection. You can even become sick. If left unmanaged, stress can eventually lead to mental illness or complete physical exhaustion.

- **Coping with stress can build your self-esteem.** When you are under stress, you often feel as if you have no control over the situation, and your self-esteem drops. By coping with stress, you do gain some control, if not over the situation, then at least over your response to it. In taking action, you gain confidence and boost your self-esteem by demonstrating to yourself that you are not helpless.
- **Coping with stress is an important tool for living successfully.** As a teenager, you confront stressful situations just as adults do. This is the time to learn how to cope with stress and to learn skills that you will use as an adult to respond to stress in a healthy manner.

Stress is brought on by perceiving a threat and reacting to it. You can learn to manage your perceptions and reactions. Coping with stress can make you a happier and healthier person.

P A R T ◇ II

WHAT CAUSES STRESS?

The causes of stress—called stressors—can come from many different sources. What causes stress for you depends on your life at home, in the community, and at school; your activities and relationships; and your own personality. If you think of something as stressful, then it is. There are some stressful situations that you can control, modify, or even eliminate, while others are beyond your control.

Change, and adjusting to change, are major sources of stress. As a teenager, you are experiencing numerous changes in your life, and many at the same time. You are in a period of transition. You need to develop new skills to cope with each change.

Your body is developing physically, and you think and feel differently than you did when you were younger.

These important physical changes mean that you have to develop a new self-image. This puts stress on the emotions as well as on the body.

You need to make decisions about school, work, and college. Events beyond your control that happen at home, at school, and in the community can disrupt your routine. It is important for you, along with your parents and teachers, to recognize when you are under stress. It is just as important to understand what is causing your stress.

In one survey, teens listed six areas that caused them the most stress: school, family problems, employment, relationships with girlfriends or boyfriends, friends, and college. Other sources of stress include violence, drinking, and unplanned pregnancy.

Stress can begin at home with conflicts between parents and teens. At school, many teens feel stressed about doing homework, taking tests, and getting into college. These everyday worries can be compounded by stress from crises such as death, divorce, and natural disasters.

Teachers, parents, family members, and peers can be sources of stress. Stress can be caused by events and also by where they take place. It can come from the way you treat your body. For instance, poor sleeping or eating habits or the use of caffeine, nicotine, or alcohol can cause stress. Stress can come from the way you think: Do you jump to conclusions or exaggerate problems? Are you self-critical? Do you have feelings of guilt?

Many of the stressors in your life cannot be avoided. However, if you recognize the stressors, you will be better able to cope with them. At times you may feel as if you will not survive the many stressors in your life. But by developing your coping skills and building your resources—and gaining experience, as well—you will survive and you will cope.

CHAPTER 2

Stress Begins at Home

Patrick and Scott, both fifteen, sat on Scott's front steps on a Saturday morning. "I can't stay long," Patrick said. "My mom wants me to wash the kitchen floor. I can't believe how she's been treating me lately. Just when I think I can be more independent, she's handing me all these rules and all this work. She's putting a lot of pressure on me to improve my grades, too. There's too much stress."

"At least your mom talks to you," Scott answered. "My mom couldn't care less about me. She has so many of her own personal problems, she can't think about mine. My dad is never around either, so I'm totally on my own. That's what I call stress."

When a group of junior high school students was asked, "What is your greatest source of stress?" their immediate answer was, "parents." A group of older teens listed family as the second biggest source of stress, with school getting the highest vote.

One of the first things you may think of as a source of stress is conflict with parents and brothers and sisters. Even if you don't spend a lot of time at home—due to classes and activities in school, an outside job, or being with friends—you are at home for part of every day. You have to interact with your parents and brothers and sisters, and this can be a source of stress.

"My biggest source of stress is my sister," says fifteen-year-old Ellis. "We're always fighting. I can't hang out at home because of her."

"I say my parents are my biggest source of stress, because of all the rules they want me to follow," says Wade, thirteen. "There's always something you have to do at home. If you don't do it right, you get criticized, and then you feel you haven't done anything at all. If you don't do your chores, you can't go out.

"My mom has set up this curfew, too. If you come in late, she gets worried. If you change your plans, sometimes you have to lie. That's stressful for me. I think I'm doing okay, but my parents want me to do better."

As a teenager, you are starting to feel a need to separate from your parents and their control. You are looking for more freedom and responsibility. That can cause conflicts that lead to stress. Often a conflict centers on a single issue, such as the use of the family car or staying out later at night.

You want to become more independent from your parents, with more responsibilities and privileges. You want your parents to think you are mature. At the same time, you want more support from your parents as you strive to succeed in school and to achieve your plans for the future.

Stress can be caused by parents putting pressure on you to succeed in school, sports, and other activities. Your parents may have certain standards of behavior they expect you to follow, standards that you and your friends do not agree with. You may feel guilty if you think that you are not living up to your parents' expectations.

"I have to keep trying to convince my mom that I'm not doing bad things," says fourteen-year-old Yusef. "She's always checking up on me, even when I stay after school for sports. She's always comparing me to my younger brother or her friend's son. We really get into some big arguments. That makes me angry and really stressed."

On the other hand, your parent's behavior may embarrass you. "There are times when I want to pretend that my dad isn't my dad," says Adam, thirteen. "He does stupid things in public, or he yells at me. It really makes me nervous."

You may think that your parents are expecting you to assume too much responsibility. You may not like helping out at home with cleaning and cooking or taking care of younger brothers and sisters. This becomes a source of conflict and stress.

Of course, stress-related problems at home can go much deeper than arguing about household chores or what time to be home at night. You and your parents may have to cope with the issues of money problems, divorce, single parenting, stepparenting, substance abuse by one or more family members, or the death or illness of a family member. If a parent loses a job or starts working after a long period of no employment, or if you have to move to a new location because of a parent's job change, these are added sources of stress for both you and your family.

Family Circumstances

Many family circumstances can add stress to your life. They may include the following:

If you are living with a single parent, he or she is under stress trying to handle the obligations of two parents. You may be asked to help with responsibilities for which you are not ready or don't feel capable. These obligations come on top of your regular schedule of school, work, activities, and friends. If your single parent is away from home a lot, there may not be someone at home with whom you can discuss your problems, making the situation even more stressful for you.

"My father ran out on us five years ago, and now my mother has to work two jobs just to pay the rent and buy food and clothes," says seventeen-year-old Julita. "I practically raised my sister. My parents weren't there when I needed them, so I don't listen to my mother anymore."

If you are a foster child, you have to live with change and uncertainty. "I've been in different foster homes all my life," says seventeen-year-old Mel. "Just like my friends, I had the stress of staying in school and staying out of gangs. I could add to that the stress of constantly adjusting to new foster homes, new people, and new rules. So I'm glad to say that I've learned to deal with it. I'm going to graduate from high school, and I even plan on attending college."

If you live in a blended family with a stepparent and stepbrothers and sisters, conflicts can arise there, too. Along with the usual problems of family life, you must add the stress of accepting a new parent and a new family, different expectations, and perhaps a different lifestyle.

If your parents are going through a divorce or separation, this is a major source of stress. "There was a lot of stress before my parents divorced, because of all the fighting," says Iris, fourteen. "Then there was the stress of the divorce itself. I had to deal with my own feelings and with my mom's feelings too. I can't understand why she was so upset about the divorce, since she and my dad never got along anyway.

"Even though the divorce is now final, there's still stress for me. When I know my parents are going to be at the same place, like Parents' Night at school, I feel sick to my stomach. I'm afraid they're going to fight in public.

"When Mom was fighting with Dad before the divorce, she couldn't pay much attention to my problems. She still can't, because now she's a single parent and she has to do her own coping."

If a close member of the family is seriously ill or has died, you are facing another powerful source of stress from a combination of strong emotions. You probably feel great sadness, fear, anger, and guilt. The rest of your family is experiencing the same emotions, so if the family does not work together to cope with this crisis, you may also feel abandoned and distant.

If there has been substance abuse (abuse of alcohol or drugs) by family members, or

If you have been the victim of sexual, emotional, or verbal abuse, you need to seek professional help, starting with school counselors or police or community social workers. (See chapter 9 for more information on getting professional help.) Never feel like you must deal with this kind of problem entirely on your own—even if other family members are telling you to keep things quiet.

When Your Parents Have Problems

Often when your parents have problems, it creates problems—and stress—for you, too. If your parent is unem-
ployed, if you have to move to another home or even lose
your home because of a bad economic situation, these are
serious sources of stress. If you have a single parent, or if
your parent is an alcoholic or a substance abuser, you may
be faced with many stressful situations. There are many
reasons for disruption in the family.

You recognize that your parent has his or her own
stresses and problems, and that adds to your stress. Your
parent may be having trouble with work, or marriage or
health problems. When parents are under stress, they can
be uncaring, violent, or overprotective. They may exaggerate, generalize, or overreact to your problems.

Sixteen-year-old Collin explains his situation: "I know
my dad's under a lot of stress because of his work. His
company is laying off a lot of people, and he doesn't know
if he's next. Whenever I do something he doesn't like,
Dad says, 'You always do that,' even if I've never done it
before. Once in a while, I'd like to talk to Dad about
things that cause me stress; I think that would help. He
seems so preoccupied and angry with his own stress,
though, that I can't talk to him."

Instead of being supportive and helping their teenagers
deal with stress, some parents are not helpful, creating
even more stress in the family. Many teens say that their
parents do not spend much time with them and do not
communicate well with them.

"My parents put a lot of pressure on me to do better in
school," says sixteen-year-old Roger. "That's where it
ends. I can't talk to them about my problems. It's frustrat-
ing and it's stressful."

Pressure to Perform

Are you trying out for a part in the school play, playing soccer in an important game next week, or hoping to get a good grade on the next math test? Are your parents telling you to improve your grades, get a job, and help out at home? You may be feeling pressured, by both yourself and your parents, to do more and to do better. Many people in our society try to "have it all." They want both personal achievement and material goods. But there is never enough physical energy, time, or money to have it all. The response is stress.

You may feel pressure from your parents to do well in school, sports, and other activities. Your parents can be very demanding, but their high expectations—in moderation, along with support and encouragement—can have a positive effect. However, when expectations become too high, the result is stress.

If you think that too many pressures or high expectations are imposed either by your parent or by yourself, it may lead to anger, frustration, or unacceptable behavior. Anger adds to stress. You need to compromise, and that calls for communication. Conflicts at home are usually the result of misunderstanding and poor communication.

Your Self-Image

Not just your family, but your own personality may cause you increased stress. How you look at yourself will influence how you view stress and how you cope with it. If you have low self-esteem or feelings of failure, you are adding to your stress and making it more difficult to deal with. When you have self-confidence, you are better able to deal with stress, and you may not even think of certain situations as stressful when others do.

Your self-image is connected to your self-esteem. Most teens are very concerned about being accepted. You are struggling with your desire to belong to the group, while at the same time wanting to be independent and do what you think is right. You may have considered joining a clique or gang to feel accepted by your peers.

Like most teens, you are probably concerned about your physical appearance. You are going through a period of physical change that may include growth spurts. It can be stressful when you don't like the way you look.

How you treat your body and how you think can influence how much stress you experience. Bad sleeping or eating habits; the use of caffeine, nicotine, alcohol, or excessive salt and sugar; or a lingering illness can all contribute to feelings of stress or weaken your ability to cope with stress. If you jump to conclusions, exaggerate problems, or make generalized statements about your behavior ("I'm *always* doing something wrong"), you will increase the amount of stress you feel.

You are also trying to maintain your own standards of behavior. You probably have your own goals and standards of achievement. If you do not reach those goals, you create stress for yourself. "I know I'm creating my own stress, but it's hard not to," says fifteen-year-old Felicia. "There are so many things I want to do besides school, like my job and cheerleading. I know I'm not getting enough sleep, and I'm not eating right. When I'm tired or hungry, the smallest thing—for instance, losing my pen—can make me feel stressed."

As you mature, you are faced with many changes in your life. You also need to make many important decisions, such as whether you should go to college or get a job. Anytime you have to make a decision, it can be stressful. You may feel stuck in your tracks, unable to do much else until you come to a conclusion; or you may rush to make a decision without giving it much thought and end up with an unwise solution or one for which you are not prepared. You have many worries that you are reluctant to share with adults such as your parents or teachers.

Talking with your friends is often a very good way of reducing stress. However, sometimes you are afraid of what your friends will think of you or that they will reject you. That leads to stress.

You will discover that one good way to cope with stress is to talk to family and friends. You need people at home to talk to, but if your parent is not at home much, is unwilling to talk, or is the source of your stress, Part III of this book will help you find other places to go.

CHAPTER 3

Stress at School

"**S**ometimes I get so stressed with school, all I can do is sit at home and cry," fifteen-year-old Jenny says. "Every teacher gives me more homework than I can handle, as if they were the only teacher I have. No matter how good my grades are, my parents tell me I should be doing better. I think I'm doing the best I can."

"I just yell at everyone when I get stressed over school," Willis, fourteen, says. "My grades are all right, but I worry more about school sports, especially soccer. My dad expects me to be a good player because he was when he was my age. Of course, I don't want to let the team down and make them lose. So I get tense, and you can't play your best unless you're relaxed."

Sixteen-year-old Margo has a different source of stress. "My mom expects me to do a lot in the music department," Margo says. "I play flute in the band and orchestra, and I have rehearsals five days a week. I take lessons, so I have to practice every day. Mom wants me to enter all these contests because it will look good on my school record. She'll never let me quit. My older sister couldn't quit until she was twenty-one. I love music, but it's really hard to fit all this in and still do my homework. I feel like I'm living in the music department. Sometimes I'd like to do something entirely different, like play tennis or something."

Like Jenny, Willis, and Margo, you can probably think of a lot of sources of stress at school. For many teens, school is the greatest source of stress in their lives, mainly from the fear of doing poorly.

There are many stressors in school, some of them not even related to schoolwork. But you will probably find that stress in school starts with schoolwork. Your problems may include homework—sometimes there's too much, sometimes it's too difficult—trying to get good grades; taking tests; worrying about failing; dealing with pressures from parents, teachers, and principals; and graduating. The causes of stress don't stop there. You may feel pressure to win and succeed in sports or music, or you may be worried about making friends and being accepted by the group. Like many teens, you probably want to look good and be popular.

ACADEMIC PERFORMANCE

The most frequent cause of stress in school is concern about academic performance and everything that goes with it, such as grades and exams. Like most teens, you are probably concerned about your grades. The goal for some teenagers is to get grades that are just good enough to pass or to graduate. For others, it is important to get higher grades for admission to college or getting a good job.

"I get pretty nervous just before report cards come out," says Peter, fourteen. "You don't know how you're going to do, after taking all those tests and writing all those papers. One time my parents had to come to school for a conference before they could pick up my report card. I was so nervous, I was actually shaking. My heart was pounding, and I couldn't even swallow. My parents were sure something was wrong. In the end, my report card wasn't too bad. Just thinking about it had me really stressed."

"I feel stressed when I have to take a test," says fifteen-year-old Katie. "I'm tired from staying up late studying for the test and doing homework for my other classes. I always get a headache. I'm so busy getting stressed that I don't do as well as I could on the test."

"Just about the time I have to take final exams in school, I always get a bad cold or sore throat," says fourteen-year-old Sam. "Mom says my resistance to disease is lower because of the stress. It's weird, but stress affects your body, not just your mind. Well, Mom ought to know, she's a doctor."

"I get the worst stress when I have to give a report in front of the whole class. I think I'm going to have a heart attack," Marina, fifteen, says. "It's funny, because I know all the kids in my class and some are good friends, but I still get dizzy and feel almost like I'm going to faint. I'm always afraid I'm going to say something stupid."

"It used to be that whenever I would take an exam, I'd be so stressed that I would be in tears," says Marina's friend, Elsa. "My grades were never very good. When I stopped worrying so much about the exams, I actually did better."

Some teens strive for perfection in their academic performance. Sixteen-year-old Greg tried that. "I was getting pretty good grades," Greg says. "But anything less than an A wasn't good enough for me. In fact, when I got As, I started trying to get A-pluses. I worked very hard, late at night, even skipped meals to study. I had a constant headache and a backache. I got really depressed, too, because I could never reach my goal of perfection.

"My parents wanted me to get good grades, but they were worried about me. They wanted me to see the school counselor. I didn't have time to see a counselor; I had to study. They kept harping on it, so I finally went. The counselor got me to set different goals. He told me what I probably already knew, but wouldn't admit to myself: Perfection is an impossible goal, because you can never reach it. I had to learn to be satisfied with good work and not try to be perfect."

Greg was putting pressure on himself to do well in school, to the point that his parents were worried. Often, it's the other way around—parents pressure their teenagers to do better in school. Like many other teens, you may feel that your parents are pressuring you too much about school.

"My parents come from the Philippines," says fourteen-year-old Anita. "They had very strict standards when they were going to school there. Now they expect me to follow the same standards. It's hard. I'm doing my best, but it never seems to be good enough. My parents even threaten to take me back to the Philippines if I don't get good grades. That's a lot of pressure and a lot of stress for me."

"My mom keeps nagging me about my grades. We're always arguing about which high school I should go to," says thirteen-year-old Dion. "I want to go to the co-ed Catholic school where most of my friends are planning to go. Mom wants me to go to the all-boys school, but she keeps threatening me that if I don't get good grades, I won't have a choice anyway. I'll just end up at the public school in my neighborhood. All this stress is giving me a constant headache."

SCHOOL ACTIVITIES

Sixteen-year-old Aaron knows that parental pressure can go beyond schoolwork and grades. "If your mom or dad were good in a sport, or your older brother or sister played that sport, your parents expect you to play it and to be good, too," Aaron says. "I'm tall like my dad, and he played basketball, so he expects me to play too. I like basketball; but when my dad comes to the game, I get so nervous, I can't play my best. After a game, Dad's always telling me what I should have done, like I should have guarded better or scored more points. He even talked to my coach about giving me more playing time; that was really embarrassing."

Cecilia, fifteen, puts a lot of pressure on herself by participating in many school activities. "Sometimes I really feel overloaded, and I can't fit everything in," Cecilia says. "I'm on the dance committee, and I'm a cheerleader. I work part time, and, of course, I've got a lot of homework. I keep saying I'm going to give something up, but what? I just end up doing more."

Fifteen-year-old Nathan says, "There are so many things in school, and you feel sort of pressured to do it all. I want to participate in sports, but I can't stay after school late because I have to study."

Teresa, seventeen, is a cheerleader. "I have practice, and I have to attend all the games, even the away games at other schools," Teresa says. "It's fun, but it's very time-consuming. I know I'm under stress because when I'm trying to study, my muscles tighten up and I get a head-ache. Sometimes I get so depressed, I want to cry. I don't feel the stress while I'm cheerleading, so how can I give that up?"

"I really don't have a life outside of school and work," says seventeen-year-old Felipe. "During the week, I go to school, and work four days a week after school. I also like track and field and basketball. Some nights I only get about three hours of sleep. I do my homework until past midnight and on the way to class. Sometimes I don't get into bed until 2:00 or 3:00 AM, and I have to get up again at six. It's really hectic; there's no time to relax."

Being involved in too many activities, rather than trying to get good grades, is often the source of stress for many teens. Or, it may be the pressure of just one activity, as in the case of Lisa and Meg.

Lisa, Meg, Howie, and Rudy had been friends since fifth grade. They lived close to each other in the city. Now that they were all in high school, they often walked home together from the bus stop.

Walking home on a crisp autumn day, the four teens couldn't stop talking about the Freshman Halloween Dance that had been held the past Saturday night.

"My mom almost forced me to ask Addie to the dance," Howie said. "When I finally called her, I thought I was going to have a heart attack. I broke out in a cold sweat, my heart was beating too hard, and I could hardly talk."

"I felt the same way when I went to the dance, and I didn't even call a girl," Rudy replied. "Just walking into the gym, I felt stressed. I kept asking myself, how do I look? Will anyone dance with me? Will anyone even talk to me? I was ready to go home until I found out almost everyone else was as nervous as I was."

"You guys had it easy," Lisa said. "Meg and I were on the planning committee, so we were stressed out weeks before the dance, worrying whether it would be a success.

We worried whether the decorations would stay up, did we buy enough food, or too much, what would we do if someone started a fight or something. I could hardly enjoy the dance."

MAJOR CHANGES

School is a big source of stress for a variety of reasons. Change is a significant source of stress, and change is taking place all the time in school. You need to cope with change, make important decisions, and set and meet new standards.

"People are always telling you to set goals; that's supposed to help you cope with stress. My goals seem to be constantly changing, so that creates stress," says sixteen-year-old Vince. "When I started the ninth grade, I moved from a small middle school in my neighborhood to a huge high school that I have to take two buses to get to. There seemed to be thousands of students, almost all of whom were older and bigger than me. All of a sudden I had more difficult classes, more homework, and more activities, too. My goal then was just to get through the ninth grade.

"Well, I did survive ninth grade, and now that I am in my third year of high school, I'm trying to get to graduation. I also have to think about what I'm going to do after graduation. Should I go to college, or go to work, or what? If I decide on college, I have to choose one, or at least find one that will take me. If I decide to go to work, I'll have the stress of finding a job.

"Like I said, my goals keep changing. I have to make a lot of decisions about those goals. Opinions and pressures are coming at me from all sides—from my parents, my teachers, my friends."

At eighteen, Ken has discovered that some decisions may cause stress in the beginning but are worth it in the long run. "The fact that I'm going to graduate is my greatest achievement. So many of my friends dropped out, and they kept pressuring me to drop out too. That may have been the easiest solution. Of course my teachers kept trying to persuade me to stay in school. It caused a lot of stress along the way. I lost a lot of sleep. I stopped eating, then I started eating too much. Now, despite all the stress, I'm glad that I stayed in school. It makes me feel good that I survived."

PEER PRESSURE

During your teen years, you are changing a great deal. You think, feel, act, and look a lot different than you did just a few years ago. You are probably still trying to establish your own identity. You are developing new skills in school—not just academic skills, but social skills as well. Most teens want to feel accepted and a part of the group.

In school and in the community, peer pressure creates a lot of stress. You may be under pressure from your friends to try alcohol or drugs, or to engage in sexual activity or generally unacceptable behavior. If any of these activities goes against what your parents have taught you, or what you yourself think, you will feel as if you are being pulled in two directions at once. Who will you go with; is there a way to compromise? This is a definite source of stress.

Getting good grades and being accepted by the group are actually in conflict for some teenagers. That's how sixteen-year-old Xavier felt. Xavier was on the junior-varsity soccer team and played touch football with friends. He was in the school play. Xavier was also doing very well in school academically. He was one of the top people in his class. "I never talk about grades or schoolwork with my friends. Getting good grades is not the way to impress them," Xavier says. "I don't want them to call me a nerd and stay away."

For fourteen-year-old Roberto, good grades and safety are tied together. "I'm lucky to be able to go to a parochial school outside of my neighborhood," he says. "But, if I don't keep my grades up, Mom might send me to the public school near my home. I wouldn't want to do that. There are too many gangs and other bad things at that school. So, that puts a lot of pressure on me to get good grades."

NEGATIVE BEHAVIOR

In some cases, school stress does not come from trying to get good grades. Instead, for some teens, it is lack of motivation. These teens are not successful academically, and they are turned off by school. They have a bad attitude and may act out violently, fighting in school to get attention, trying to be part of the group through violence, or joining friends in crime to feel that they belong. This negative behavior usually leads to other problems, such as anxiety, stress, and depression.

"I dread to see my teachers. I'm just not motivated," says Larissa, fourteen.

Fifteen-year-old Natalie says, "I have a friend who wasn't doing too well in school. She was getting so much pressure from her parents to get better grades, she was thinking about suicide. 'I really don't care anymore. Life might as well be over,' she told me. That scared me so much, I had to tell the school counselor. I'm happy to say that my friend worked everything out, and she's doing much better now."

EXTERNAL PRESSURES

Some things that were once problems only of the wider world and the problems of adults have now come into the school and are sources of stress for teenagers. Many teens must now deal with the death of a classmate by murder, accident, or suicide. Students are carrying weapons such as knives and guns into school. You, or others you know, may be cheating on tests. In many schools, drugs and alcohol are being used. Many of the stressors occurring in school these days used to be found only in the "outside world," outside the home and school. But just as stress does not stop at the walls of your home, it doesn't stop at the walls of the school, either.

CHAPTER 4

Stress from the Outside

Ephram couldn't figure out which was more stressful: being a freshman in high school, or walking home after school. He passed tough-looking gang members—in school, everyone called them "gangbangers"—who were hanging around the school as he walked home. "All those guys dropped out a long time ago," Ephram told his friend Roy. "How come they show up at the playground every day?"

The gang members alternated between taunting Ephram because he was still going to school and sweet-talking him to get him to join the gang. This worried Ephram. He knew about other boys his age or even younger who had been shot for not belonging to a gang or for belonging to the wrong one.

Ephram has discovered that where you live may have a lot to do with how much stress there is in your life. Along with the usual stressors teens face, teens who live in areas where they must deal with gangs and violence experience a lot of stress resulting from fear, violence, and pressure from gangs. Just living from day to day can be a challenge for some teens. Problems like these are making their way into all parts of the cities, and into the suburbs as well.

Gangs are now found in every area of the country: rural areas, small towns, and suburbs, as well as inner-city areas. However, according to high school counselors, inner-city teens still experience stress unique to their environment.

If there are gangs in your town or neighborhood, it creates a whole new set of stressors for you and your friends. "There's so much pressure put on you to join a gang," says Richard, seventeen. "Probably the easiest way is to join one. But you could end up dead the next week. Or you could try to survive without joining a gang and end up dead anyway. It happened to my friend Harris. We were planning to graduate together next May, but he was shot last week, just walking home from school. How do you think that makes me feel?

"I have another friend, Trace, who isn't sure about the gangs. He's not really a member of any gang, but he dresses like some of the gang members and sort of hangs out with them. But, he could get into trouble too, with the police or with members of a rival gang."

CRIME AND VIOLENCE

In many communities, the greatest source of stress is crime and violence and the fear of crime and violence. Many teenagers have been either the victim of a crime or know someone who has. Often, both the attacker and the victim are teenagers. Crime and violence are daily occurrences in some communities. Teenagers who experience this daily stress are more susceptible to developing symptoms such as anxiety and fear.

Luann, thirteen, says, "I'm afraid to walk to the next building in my project because I might get shot by a gang member."

People living in the midst of urban violence continually have to adjust to threats of death and violence while still trying to maintain their everyday existence. The stress is so great that some even suffer the traumatic symptoms of having survived a war or a natural disaster; they develop symptoms such as fear, anxiety, irritability, depression, abdominal pain, chest pain, headache, and sweating. Teens exposed to this chronic stress may react by acting out or joining a gang. Teenagers living in an urban setting are also subject to stress from poverty and racism.

Most teenagers, even those living in wealthy areas, say that they worry about crime. Fear of crime can be just as stressful as being the actual victim of a crime.

"So many bad things happen in my neighborhood, you become afraid of everything," says sixteen-year-old Wanda. "Just going to the corner store can be stressful. My heart beats faster, my hands start to sweat, even if there's no one around. Last week, I was only going to the store to pick up a carton of milk for Mom, when this weird-looking guy started to follow me. I never got to the store. I crossed the street and ran all the way home. It must have taken fifteen minutes for my heart to slow down."

"I'm never sure how to act with the police," sixteen-year-old Marshall says. "Sometimes they act as if you're the criminal, when you haven't done anything. Other times they can help you out of a tough situation. If too many kids get together, the police break them up. In our neighborhood, we can't even cruise anymore. That used to be our whole Saturday night. I know there are some police who treat kids disrespectfully, but I'm usually glad to see the police."

Brian, fifteen, points out that violence is not the only source of stress for people living in the city. "There are too many crowds. Even our classrooms are crowded. Everyone is in a hurry. They'll knock you down if you get in the way, even if they're in a car," Brian says. "And don't forget about noise and dirt and pollution. Sometimes I feel like I'm living in a dungeon with no escape. I try to do what I can, like recycling cans and bottles and papers, and helping our church group clean up around the neighborhood. But there are still so many things that I can't change."

SOCIAL PROBLEMS

Dealing with prejudice and racism can be a source of stress. All people need to have friends and want to be accepted, but you may have found yourself in a situation where you have been rejected—in either a subtle or obvious way—because of a mental or physical disability, your age, race, or other personal characteristics.

"It's really stressful when people stereotype you," says fifteen-year-old Eric. "I mean, they think you can't do something well just because of your race or ethnic background. It really gets me mad. I'm trying to do my best and someone comes along and says, 'Oh, you must have cheated, you can't do work that good.'"

"I know what Eric means," says Nina, fourteen. "Whenever I go into this clothing store, someone immediately starts to follow me around the store. I'm sure it's because I'm Hispanic. Going into that store makes me so nervous.

"One day, when I went into that store with some friends, a salesperson started to follow us. Finally, I decided to call her bluff. I said, 'Do you think I'm stealing? Go ahead and search me.' Well, she didn't search me, but she didn't bother me after that, either."

"Even some of my friends have racist views," Eric adds. "It really makes me uncomfortable when they put down people behind their backs. They don't realize they're insulting me, too. It makes me wonder what they say behind my back."

Fifteen-year-old Hannah agrees. "When I'm with someone making anti-Semitic remarks, I try not to let them know I'm Jewish. That can be very stressful."

Nina laughs. "That's great for you, but if you're black or Hispanic, you can't hide it. People know it right away."

"People discriminate against me because I have long hair and earrings," says sixteen-year-old Mark.

"And I'm discriminated against because I'm Arab," says Jamilah, fourteen. "Especially after a terrorist attack, kids at school ask if one of my relatives did it. Well, I'm just as afraid of the terrorists as anyone. That just doubles my stress."

FEELING OUT OF CONTROL

Feeling as if you have no control over sources of stress becomes a cause of stress itself. In fact, those unable to cope with problems in their lives and in their community, such as drugs, violence, and pollution, may experience severe stress, which can lead to depression and even suicide.

You don't have to be a victim of a crime to experience stress. Simply witnessing something upsetting can be an emotional shock. Observing the death or illness of a friend or family member, seeing one parent abuse the other, or even watching upsetting news on television can cause real stress. Because, through television, you can see firsthand the results of war and hatred in distant parts of the world, it may cause you to overestimate the amount of violence in the world.

Since many of these problems are not under our control, it creates feelings of insecurity. Divorce, moving, unemployment, or a lack of feeling of permanence can all give you the feeling that you are not in control of your life. Feeling out of control can cause stress.

We are also getting cues from the media on how we are supposed to look and what we should be doing. It's a fast-paced world where there is pressure to achieve, look good, and be successful. Money seems to be tied into everything, so it hurts if you don't have it.

FITTING IN

For you, the problems causing stress may not be as threatening to your well-being as those of other teens, but your feelings of stress are just as strong. Like most teens, you probably want to feel that you "belong." You want to have friends; you want to feel good about yourself. When these things don't happen, you may feel angry, frustrated, or depressed; these are emotions that can lead to stress.

Thirteen-year-old Michael was always worried about friends: Who were his friends? Did they like him? What did they say about him behind his back?

Michael wanted to give a party, but he kept putting off sending the invitations because he was afraid no one would come. "If you don't send those invitations soon, it will be too late. No one will be able to come," his mother warned him. Michael did send out the invitations, and most of his friends said they would come.

On the day of the party, Michael felt sick. He had a stomachache, and he couldn't eat breakfast. He hadn't slept all night. Now he was worried people wouldn't show up at his party anyway, and if they did, they wouldn't have a good time. "I'm sick," he told his mother. "I'd better call the party off."

"Don't be silly," his mother answered. "You're just nervous." Michael didn't call the party off. Except for one person, everyone who said they would come did come, and Michael thought they had a good time. "Yeah, the party was okay," he told a friend later. "But, I'll never have a party again; it was just too stressful!"

DATING AND SEXUAL PRESSURE

"My mom is always putting pressure on me about dating," says Beth, fourteen. "She tells me I'm too young to date. I'm not really dating. I just want to go out with my friends. Sometimes we just go to someone's house and hang out. Once in a while we like to ride around in one of the guys' cars. That's when Mom really blows up.

"Mom's probably worried that I'm going to have sex on a date. On the one hand, there's Mom saying 'Don't have sex,' and on the other hand, my friends tease me because I'm still a virgin."

Sixteen-year-old Rolando explains: "There's a lot of pressure to have sex, even in junior high school. People tease you if you are a virgin. Once you do it, you feel like the pressure is off."

Having a relationship with someone may be a new experience for you. Just like any other change in your life, that can be a source of stress. You wonder how to act and what to do. What's appropriate? What's expected? Are you acting too shy or too aggressive? How do your parents react to the situation?

You may hear older friends, brothers, or sisters talk about having sex on a date, drinking, or doing other things that you are not sure you want to do or are ready to do. Television, movies, and even popular music may make you think you need to be sexually active to be popular. This puts a lot of pressure on you. It's probably not a subject you want to discuss with others, especially your parents.

"Whether or not to have sex can really cause a lot of stress," says Marci, fifteen. "You get pressure from your parents; you get pressure from your friends. Add to that the fear of getting AIDS or other diseases or getting pregnant. Some of my friends worry more about getting pregnant than getting AIDS. We all know that the best prevention is abstinence, but it's hard not to have sex when we see and hear so much about it in music, on television, and in the movies. And what about our hormones? Our bodies are telling us to have sex, too!"

At sixteen, Paco had always been shy around girls. One Saturday night, he went with some friends to a party in the neighborhood. Paco met Marla at the party. They talked a lot and danced a little. Paco liked Marla, and he decided he wanted to go on a date with her. As Paco tried to work up the courage to ask Marla out, his stomach started churning, his heart rate grew faster, and he started to sweat. The whole time, Paco tried to appear calm and talk casually as if he had asked hundreds of girls out already.

Paco's stomach and heart didn't seem to calm down the whole week before his date with Marla. In fact, things got worse. Now Paco was worried about the date. Should he have sex with Marla? Would she expect it? Paco was getting mixed messages. He knew that his older brother and many of his friends had already had sex with their girlfriends—at least that's what they told him. On the other hand, his teachers and priest kept warning the kids that sex before marriage was not only immoral, but might lead to some bad diseases like AIDS and, of course, unwanted pregnancies.

The night before his date, Paco couldn't eat, even though his mother had fixed his favorite meal. "I don't understand you, Paco," his mother said. "You're getting all upset about this date. It's only a date."

Paco couldn't explain anything to his mother. But he could talk to his older brother, J.J. It seemed as if J.J. was always there for Paco. Even if J.J. did things that Paco didn't agree with, J.J. was great at listening. Sometimes, just talking to J.J. was all that Paco needed to make up his own mind about some problem.

Stress about sex and dating is normal. It's also normal to be stressed out about the fact that you're *not* dating right now.

TROUBLE WITH OTHER TEENS

Psychologists say that it is important for people to have some close personal relationships. In fact, a close relationship—whether it is with a friend or relative—is one way of coping with stress. However, your desire for a close friendship may conflict with your striving to be independent. This can cause stress. You may have a conflict between wanting to be like your friends and wanting to be different. You want to be close to your friends, yet you are afraid of rejection.

As a teen, you are seeking acceptance by your friends, especially friends that you are attracted to sexually. This can put pressure on you and be quite stressful. In your effort to be accepted, your behavior might lead to even more serious stress-producing consequences, such as pregnancy or crime.

"Everyone wants to be accepted by others," says Zoe, sixteen. "That puts a lot of pressure on you and creates a lot of stress. Teens feel they have to be just like the other kids. They're scared to be themselves. If you're different, you won't be popular."

If some of your friends commit crimes, drink alcohol, use drugs, or engage in any other activity that you feel is wrong, you have some serious stress-producing problems to deal with. First, you must consider how your friends' behaviors influence your own behavior. Do you go along with them, even though you believe that what they are doing is wrong? Do you reject their behavior and perhaps risk losing their friendship? Or do you go even further than that and report their illegal behavior?

A police youth worker says that teens often get in trouble with the law because of peer pressure.

Fourteen-year-old Gail was confused about her relationship with Maria and Jackie. The three girls had been friends since they were in the seventh grade together. To Gail, Maria and Jackie seemed very grown up. They were the first in their class to wear makeup and the first to go on dates instead of going out with a group or to a party. They were friendly to Gail, and she liked that because she didn't have a lot of friends.

Often Gail got together after school with the other two girls. Gail didn't talk a lot, but listened. Gradually, through their conversation, Maria and Jackie revealed that they were shoplifting makeup, jewelry, and clothes from the mall. They even invited Gail to join them on their next "shopping spree." Gail tried to refuse politely. She did not want to get caught—it wasn't worth it.

Gail began to feel more and more tension and stress when she was with Maria and Jackie. She wanted to continue to be their friend. She didn't want to be a snitch.

She decided to keep their secret, even though she didn't like what they were doing.

After she found out about the shoplifting, Gail started to have headaches and stomachaches. Sometimes she couldn't concentrate on doing her homework, or couldn't sleep because she was worried that someone would find out about her friends' stealing, and she would be blamed for telling.

Gail decided to spend less time with the two girls, but she also noticed that they were making excuses not to include her in their plans as well. Eventually, Gail made friends with other girls who didn't want to associate with Maria and Jackie either.

Maybe you are not as worried about your own behavior as you are about your friends' behavior. You may sometimes feel embarrassed for a friend, or embarrassed to be with that friend.

"I really get annoyed with one of my friends," says fifteen-year-old Lance. "He's a real showoff. Sometimes he will do the stupidest things just to get attention. Then my other friends tell me I shouldn't hang around with him. When he gets in trouble with the teachers, they tell me to stay away from him or I'll get in trouble too.

"But I can't drop him as a friend. I've known him my whole life. We live in the same apartment building. He needs me to be his friend. If I dropped him, he would feel terrible. And, I'd feel terrible too; worse than I do when others tease me about being his friend. It's a real problem for me."

Some teens join cliques or gangs to get the acceptance they don't find at home. Ben, fourteen, was lonely and wanted to have some friends. A few of the older boys in the high school, some of whom were in gangs, took advantage of Ben. They were friendly, making him feel like a part of the group. Then they started asking him to do things that he thought were wrong. Ben felt more stress than before, because he had to decide whether to follow his conscience or do what the guys wanted. He was also afraid that they might hurt him if he refused to do what they wanted.

Sylvie didn't want to lose her boyfriend, so she went along with his pressure to have sex. Soon Sylvie was fearful that she might get pregnant, or develop AIDS or another sexually transmitted disease. The stress from this worry caused Sylvie to have stomachaches. Sylvie thought the stomachaches meant she really was sick, so it only compounded the problem.

Because you are a maturing teen, you are expected to start taking control of your life. Others have high expectations of you. You are expected to take responsibility for your actions. You are now becoming a part of the community. You may be moving out of your parents' home, getting a job, or both. These changes can produce a lot of stress.

STRESS ON THE JOB

There are many ways your employment can cause you stress: if you need a job and have to look for one; if you're afraid of losing the job you already have; if your job takes up too much of your time; or if there is too much pressure put on you by your employer or your parents to succeed in your job.

Sixteen-year-old Sven says, "It's hard for a teen to get a decent job because of the economic situation. But some people just think we're lazy."

If you have a job, you may experience a lot of stress there, too. You may feel some conflict with your supervisor or your coworkers. There may be a lot of competition or very high standards. You may also have a problem with your working conditions. If there is too much noise, if your workspace is too small or too isolated, or if you are working with toxic materials, for example, your job can be very stressful.

"I really get worried when I'm at my job," says sixteen-year-old Hassan. "I work in a small factory, and I'm always reading about how dangerous chemicals and air pollution in a factory can make you sick."

"I help out in my dad's store after school," says Michael, seventeen. "There have been a lot of store robberies lately. I wonder when it is going to happen to us. Sometimes I worry so much, I start to feel sick. Then I don't even want to work in the store anymore. But I know Dad needs the help. It would be worse if he had to work alone."

Change is taking place in your community and in the world. You are experiencing many changes firsthand. You must make decisions about finishing high school, going to college or going to work, and even whether to move out of your parents' home and start out on your own. You are meeting rising expectations. There is a lot of pressure on you and other teens not just to get by, but to achieve and be successful. You have to deal with these changes as well as cope with problems such as crime, racism, and personal relationships. The result is stress.

CHAPTER 5

Critical Conditions:
Crises and Disasters

"I was never so embarrassed in my whole life," fifteen-year-old Jessie told her friend Pam. "I went to Ken's party last night. I was having a great time, and then suddenly I felt so dizzy, I almost fainted. I had to sit down quickly and put my head down. Ken's mom told me to lie down on her bed, and she gave me a wet washcloth for my forehead. She was really nice, and all the kids seemed to feel sorry for me, but it still was so embarrassing.

"Ken's mom thought I was under stress because of my dad's illness. Maybe she's right. When Dad went into the hospital, things were really turned upside-down. Mom had to visit Dad every day and still go to work. I had to help out more at home, and it was hard to have time for my homework. I felt like there was too much pressure on me. We were all scared because for a while we weren't sure Dad was going to live or die.

"Dad was in the hospital for so many weeks, I thought he might never come home. He was finally well enough to come home a few days ago. It's great to have him here, but everything is disorganized right now because he still needs medical care. On the night of the party, I thought I should stay with Dad, but he told me to go, that I didn't have to stay with him so much. Thinking everything would be all right, I went to the party. I guess I was still thinking about Dad, though."

The illness of Jessie's dad and all the changes associated with it have created a crisis in Jessie's life. Jessie is now responding with the symptoms of stress. A crisis is a turning point in your life; a time of decision or the result of a decision; and a time of change. A crisis will almost always cause stress.

CRISES

Crises appear in a variety of forms and cause varying amounts of stress. What is known as a crisis is not always a bad situation. It may be a positive event in your life, such as recovering from an illness, graduating from school, or going on vacation. A crisis may also arise at the loss of a relationship, such as a divorce or the death of a family member or friend. It can be a situation with long-lasting results, including a long illness, an accident, the loss of a job, or a natural disaster. Of course, there will be more stress resulting from your parents' divorce than from going on vacation.

Other stress-producing crises include:

- Pregnancy or abortion
- A serious injury
- Moving
- Changing schools
- Breaking up with a boyfriend or girlfriend

- You or your parent getting a job or losing a job
- The birth of a brother or sister
- Starting or finishing school
- Your parent getting remarried
- An encounter with police
- Witnessing or being a victim of a crime
- A parent leaving the household
- Financial loss or gain
- A relative moving into your home
- Leaving home
- Going on vacation
- Celebrating the holidays
- Any change in activities, habits, or lifestyle

LOSING A FAMILY MEMBER

Probably one of the most stressful crises in a person's life is the death of a close relative, such as a parent or a brother or sister, or of a close friend. The situation can cause a variety of emotions that result in stress. You may experience depression or great sadness at the loss. At the same time, you may feel angry with other members of your family, with the person who has died for abandoning you, or with God for "taking" that person. You also may feel guilty, asking yourself if in some way you may have caused the death or could have prevented it. You may feel helpless because you could not do anything to prevent the death. Feeling that you are not in control is often a source of stress.

In school and with your friends, you may feel singled out because of their sympathy for you following a death. You may feel left out because some people don't know how to relate to someone who has experienced a death in the family. If the death was the result of AIDS, murder, or suicide, it is possible that you may feel a certain amount of shame as well as sadness about the death. You may not want to discuss it with others, which can add to your stress.

Loss of a Sibling

The death of a brother or sister can produce mixed feelings, depending on your relationship. Often a relationship with a brother or sister is a combination of affection, anger, and annoyance. Relationships among brothers and sisters differ greatly between families, depending on the difference in your ages, whether you are the same sex or not, and other factors. You and your brother or sister may not have been any closer than two unrelated people living in the same household. On the other hand, your sister or brother may have been a friend; someone you could talk to and learn from or teach; someone you competed with or argued with, yet who was an ally in disagreements with your parents. Either way, that brother or sister was a constant in your life, and losing him or her can be very stressful.

"My little sister, Cheryl, used to annoy me so much. She would come into my room and touch my stuff, even though I yelled at her all the time," says Wayne, fourteen. "One day she broke the wing on a model plane I had been working on for months. I got so mad at her, I told her I wished she would disappear forever.

"Just a few weeks later, my sister died in an accident. I was very sad about her death, but I also was frightened. Did what I said cause her death? I got very depressed thinking about it. I couldn't eat or sleep. I just wanted to lie on my bed in a dark room and not do anything. I had a constant headache, and my heart seemed to be beating too fast.

"My parents were upset about my sister's death, but I know that they were worried about me too. They sent me to a therapist, and she helped me work out my feelings so I could cope better."

If you have just one brother or sister, after his or her death you become an only child. Not only have you lost someone who may have been a friend and an ally, but now your parents may start treating you in an overprotective manner. They don't want anything to happen to you; they don't want to lose you, too. This adds one more pressure to an already stressful situation.

Your parent's grief from losing a child or a spouse may be so overwhelming that he or she cannot comfort or help you. You may begin to feel as if you have lost a parent as well as the person who died.

Sixteen-year-old Gretta says, "I was devastated when my sister, Danielle, died in a bicycle accident last year. She was two years younger than me. Our family was very close. In fact, we did a lot of bike riding together, so it's sort of ironic that bike riding was what tore our family apart.

"I know I'll never really get over Danielle's death. I'll always miss her. I sure went through a lot of emotions after she died. Sometimes I felt so weak and dizzy, I thought I was going to die, too. I couldn't eat, and I couldn't sleep. I often felt guilty; maybe I could have prevented Danielle's death if I had gone on that trip with her.

"It's a good thing my teacher suggested I see a counselor, because I really needed someone to talk to. Usually my parents are there for me when I have a problem, but not after Danielle's accident. My parents were so upset, they were out of control, too. At first, they almost ignored me. I wanted to say, 'Hey, remember me? I'm your daughter, too.' I'm glad my Aunt Viv was there to comfort me.

"A few weeks after the accident, my mom started paying *too* much attention to me. She was afraid to let me go bike riding; she was afraid to let me do practically anything. She didn't even want me to get my driver's license, because she didn't want me to get into a car accident. I know she didn't want to lose me, too, but I needed to get back to living my life.

"My dad was just the opposite. After Danielle died, Dad seemed to withdraw from life. He just went to work and went to sleep. He didn't pay any attention at all to me. He didn't ride his bike anymore. My counselor told me Dad is just taking a longer time to work through his grief than it took Mom and me. In the meantime, I feel like I've lost a father as well as a sister. I feel as if I have to cope with my parents' stress as well as my own stress."

You may grieve for a long time after someone has died. "Two years after my brother Brian died, I had a fight with my best friend, Anna," Laura, thirteen, says. "On my way home I thought, Brian will know how to handle this. But then I remembered Brian wasn't there anymore, and I just stood there on the street and started to cry. I don't know when I'll get over Brian's death."

DIVORCE

When your parents decide to separate or get a divorce, this situation may become a stressful crisis in your life. The divorce itself, as well as the problems that caused the divorce in the first place, can be sources of stress. You may respond to the stress with a variety of symptoms.

After her parents' divorce, fourteen-year-old Sonia gained a lot of weight, and her grades went down. "I guess

I stopped paying attention in class. Every time I started something, I'd think about the divorce, and I couldn't do any work," Sonia says. "Instead of doing my homework, I would go to the kitchen and eat a whole bag of potato chips or a carton of ice cream. It would make me feel better for a little while, but it didn't really change the stress I felt. It just made me fat."

"I guess at first I didn't realize how stressed I was about my parents' divorce," says Alan, fifteen. "I was depressed in school; I wasn't doing the work, and my grades were slipping. I got into a lot of arguments and even some fights, which I had never done before. I kept trying to convince myself that Mom and Dad really weren't going to get a divorce; I told myself it was just another one of their fights, and they would get back together. Then I started getting terrible stomachaches."

The divorce of your parents can cause a variety of stressful situations. You may not see a parent as often as you would like. The parent you are living with may be working harder, and may be more tired and have less time for you than before the divorce. There may be money worries. If your parent remarries, you have to adjust to your new stepparent and perhaps stepsisters and brothers.

You may feel as if you are caught in the middle, with each parent trying to get you on their side, trying to turn you against your other parent. There may be problems deciding custody, as there were for thirteen-year-old Andre. "My parents really fought about who would get custody of me and my sisters," Andre says. "A judge finally had to tell them what to do, so now we're all with my mom. It was stressful during the custody hearings. I kept wishing Mom would give Dad another chance. Now it's still stressful because Mom and I argue a lot. I sometimes think that life would be easier if I lived with Dad. The truth is that it would be even more stressful, because the only time Dad pays attention to me, he is either yelling at me or criticizing me.

"My friend Nick lives with his mother during the school year and goes to live with his dad during the summer. That's tough, too, because he has to leave his friends and even his brother all summer."

One of the most stressful factors in a divorce can be your guilty feelings that you caused the divorce, even if your parents tell you otherwise. "I thought my parents' divorce was my fault," says fourteen-year-old Martin.

If your parent is having emotional problems with the divorce, that can create added stress for you. Hannah, sixteen, felt that way. 'My mother got so emotional about the divorce; one minute she was angry, the next she was depressed. She wasn't there for me when I was trying to sort out my own feelings, and I almost had to start taking care of her. I had to ask myself, what do I want Mom to do for me? The answer was, I wanted her to be there to listen when I talked about my feelings. So I tried to listen to her, and eventually it helped both of us."

"Dad was usually on my side. Now that he's not living here anymore, I have to do everything Mom's way," says Tito, thirteen. "That makes my life even harder. As if I didn't have enough stress, Mom is getting married again. She's marrying a man with two little kids, so I'm going to have a stepfather and two stepsisters."

"My parents are divorced, but I get the most stress when they have to get together for my sake—like for Parents' Day at school or when I'm in a play," says sixteen-year-old Ingrid. "My heart starts to beat faster, and I get a dry mouth and a headache. I know it's not all stage fright; it's 'divorced parents fright!'"

PREGNANCY

By definition, pregnancy is a crisis for any woman and her family. In many cases, it is a positive crisis. However, for an unwed teenager, pregnancy can be an especially stressful situation. "A teen who finds out she is pregnant is never happy, no matter how she deals with it," says a counselor who works with teenage girls. With a pregnancy come many changes and decisions, sometimes faced by the expectant mother alone. She may feel anxiety, fear, and shame.

The man who shares responsibility for the pregnancy may also feel significant stress. This new situation has the potential to change his life as well as that of the woman. He may feel pressure to get married, or he may not acknowledge his role in the situation. Whatever his feelings are, he will have to make decisions that affect his own life and his relationship with the woman.

The only sure method of preventing pregnancy is simply to avoid having a sexual relationship. But there is a lot of pressure on teens to have sex. Television, movies, and popular music often emphasize sex. Sometimes it seems like the kids who have sex are more popular. On one side, you may be getting pressured from friends and from your own body to have sex. On the other side, you probably feel pressure from your parents and other adults to abstain from sex. And you might not feel ready to have sex, either.

JOB STATUS

Employment and unemployment are situations that can create big changes in your life and can cause stress. When you get a new job, or if you lose the job you have, you need to make adjustments in your life.

"For the first three months after I got an after-school job helping in the library, I had a constant sore throat," says sixteen-year-old Marisol. "Dad says it was stress because it was a new job. The same thing happened to Mom when she went to teach at a new school this year, and she has been teaching for ten years."

If a parent who has been working must stop because of a layoff, illness, or by choice, or if a parent goes back to work after not working for a long period of time, changes have to be made. The situation can cause stress for you as well as for your parent. Your parent's attitude may change, for better or worse. You may have to take on responsibilities that you were never asked to do before, such as getting dinner ready or watching a younger brother or sister after school. Your parents may not have as much money.

"A few months ago, my dad's company merged with another company, and my dad was laid off. He was really upset about it, really angry," says Eddie, fifteen. "When he wasn't just sitting and staring out the window, he was yelling at Mom, my sister, and me. Mom said he was under a lot of stress. Well, his stress was causing *me* stress. I was getting headaches and stomachaches. My teachers started to tell me I wasn't paying attention in class.

"We had to cut way back on our spending. I couldn't even go to the movies with my friends anymore. Then Mom started working more hours to help with everyday expenses. That was even more stressful for me. I felt like I was living with two stressed-out adults and there was no one to help me with my own stress. I didn't want to talk about it with my friends. Most of their dads were working, so I felt sort of weird because my dad's not working."

DISASTERS

Disasters include some of the most stressful events that can happen to a person and a community. They go beyond crises. A disaster may be considered a group of crises happening suddenly and all at once. Disasters may be natural or human-made and include floods, hurricanes, tornadoes, earthquakes, and fires. In today's world, disasters may also include chemical and toxic waste spills, airplane crashes, or terrorist attacks.

The immediate impact of a disaster may be death and injury, loss of home and other possessions, loss of community services, and relocation and separation of families. You may be separated from friends or family, or have to live in a different area. Any of these factors can be stressors by themselves, but in a disaster they may all affect you at once.

It may take many months or even years to recover from the losses you suffer in a disaster. In the meantime, you may feel stress from emotions such as grief over the death of family and friends, guilt for surviving when others did not, fear, loss, helplessness, or abandonment. You or your family may even have to deal with the stress of going to court when charging someone with the responsibility of causing the disaster. News of a disaster is going to appear on television and in newspapers and magazines. You may not be able to get away from reminders, which makes it more difficult to deal with your feelings and reduce your stress.

During and after a disastrous event, the fight-or-flight reaction that usually causes you stress can help you to survive the disaster and allow you to assist others. Sometimes, immediately following a disaster, if you and your family have survived and avoided death and destruction, there is a feeling of calm. Then disillusionment can set in, as you begin to realize the extent of your losses. You may experience anger and grief, and feel a loss of support, especially if you think a federal agency or insurance company that is supposed to help is not acting fast enough.

People who survive a disaster such as an earthquake may experience a variety of stress responses. Following a disaster, some people start talking about memories of traumatic situations that happened in the past. The event may stir up past feelings that have been held in for years. When you express your feelings about the disaster, you may also express your feelings about these past experiences.

"At first, I didn't want to talk to anyone about the hurricane," says sixteen-year-old Karina. "No one in our family was hurt, and I was glad about that. But our house was destroyed. Just thinking about it made me dizzy and sick to my stomach. I just wanted to crawl away somewhere and be by myself. There was a Red Cross mental health worker who finally convinced me that it would be better for me if I talked about the disaster.

"Once I started talking, I couldn't stop. All of a sudden, all these things that have bothered me in the past came spilling out, even the time the babysitter hurt me. These were things that I tried not to think about and had almost forgotten. It was hard to talk, because it brought back the bad feelings. But, after talking, I felt relieved, and it did help to reduce the stress I have felt for so long."

LIFE AFTER A DISASTER

As a teen, you are always trying to cope with a variety of stressful issues, such as problems in your family, in school, and in the community; and problems with friends, sexual relationships, and substance abuse. You may be concerned about economic issues such as money and housing. You and your family may already be dealing with divorce, illness, or death. These problems don't disappear when a disaster occurs, but are sometimes made worse.

When you survive a disaster, stressful feelings come from the loss of normalcy. Many of the things you take for granted—such as the senior prom—cannot take place. What was once a normal situation becomes abnormal.

"After the tornado hit our neighborhood, it felt like we were living on another planet, just like in *The Wizard of Oz*," says Paul, sixteen. "At least, nobody was hurt, although we worried at first because we couldn't find everyone. They set up a shelter at the high school where we could eat and sleep until our house was safe to live in. I missed sleeping in my own bed and eating regular meals. We couldn't go to the mall or the movies because our car was wrecked.

"The longer we stayed at the shelter, the more depressed I got. When we could live in our house again, it was such a mess, I got even more depressed. I didn't want to do any of the things I used to like to do. If there was just a little wind or a loud noise, my heart would start to pound. Just a warning of a storm would make me stressed. Luckily my friends didn't tease me for acting like a baby. They seemed to understand how I felt, even though the tornado hadn't hit their own neighborhoods. My friends and the school counselor really helped me get through this."

Post-Traumatic Stress Disorder

Some crises, such as a serious automobile accident or a fire, may cause an extreme stress response known as post-traumatic stress disorder. Symptoms include loss of sleep; nightmares; a mental replaying of the disaster, escape, and survival; and emotions such as guilt, anger, fear, and helplessness. This stress response is common following a natural or human-made disaster.

EXPECTING A DISASTER

The waiting time between the warning of a disaster and the actual event, even if it never occurs, can be stressful. Angela, sixteen, says, "I live near Los Angeles. They keep telling us that someday there's going to be this massive earthquake that destroys California. Every time I feel a little rumble, I tense up. I'm afraid it's going to be the 'big one,' and I'll never see my family again."

Whether you have been involved in a disaster or know someone who has, or if you have only seen disasters reported on the news, anxiety and fear of future disasters can cause stress. After the federal building in Oklahoma City was bombed in 1995, many people were afraid to go into any federal building.

"The Oklahoma bombing really scared me," says thirteen-year-old Bettina, who lives in another state. "My dad works in the federal building across the street from my school. How do I know that some crazy person isn't going to blow up his building too? Just worrying about it gives me a lot of stress."

Some people may deny the possibility of a disaster, especially a natural disaster, because they want to avoid the stress this might cause. They may ignore warnings and not take even simple precautions. However, preparing for a disaster or doing something to reduce the risk of a disaster gives you a sense of control and can help reduce stress.

"I live near a large forest, and there have been bad forest fires the last few summers," says Caitlin, fourteen. "I started having nightmares about our house burning down. I talked to my dad about it. He calmed me down a lot. He showed me where the smoke detector in our house is, and together we installed a sprinkler system. We also practiced a fire drill with the whole family. Now, even though I can't stop a fire from happening, I feel better about facing it if it happens."

In a crisis or disaster, you want to behave like an adult, but you still feel insecurity and fear. You may not want to show feelings such as guilt or grief because you think of them as "childish" reactions. However, as a teen, your reaction to a disaster is much the same as that of an adult. Adults have the same feelings of helplessness and lack of control. You go through the same anxiety and tension leading to stress as adults do. Because you have less experience dealing with this type of situation, you may need others to help you put the situation into perspective.

P A R T ◇ III

COPING WITH STRESS

There are many different sources of stress in your life. Your life cannot be totally stress-free, and you probably wouldn't want it to be. However, because unmanaged stress can lead to serious physical and emotional problems, you do need to cope with the stress you have, manage it, and reduce it.

In order to cope with stress, you, your parents, and other adults in your life should be aware of the symptoms of stress and accept that you are under stress. The next step is to find the source of your stress. Your stress can come from home and family; school; friends; relationships; crime and violence; crises such as death, divorce, and pregnancy; and disasters.

A variety of techniques help you cope with stress. You use your mind to help your cope when you solve problems, set goals, and get organized. You can think positively and keep everything in perspective. You use your body to cope when you adopt a healthy lifestyle and learn to relax. Having the support of—and being able to communicate with—family and friends is critical in coping with stress. Other adults, such as relatives, counselors, therapists, and members of the clergy, as well as support groups, may help you to deal with the pressures you feel. On the other hand, you don't want to try coping with stress by using drugs, tobacco, or alcohol, or by withdrawing from people or turning to violent behavior. These behaviors may make you feel better at first, but they will lead to more problems, and will keep you from developing the coping skills that will enable you to deal with future stressors.

Although you are still young, you can use past experience as a guideline for coping. What has worked in the past and what has not? Accept that you can't solve every problem. Take into account your own physical and emotional limitations and have reasonable expectations.

CHAPTER 6

Talking to Yourself: Using Your Mind to Cope with Stress

Daniel is a senior in high school and a very busy person. Besides attending classes—some of which are accelerated—he is codirector of the school musical and assistant manager of the junior varsity basketball team. On top of that, Daniel volunteers twice a week at the animal hospital because he wants to be a veterinarian.

"When I get home in the evening, my parents and my little brother have already had dinner," Daniel says. "I'm not usually hungry anyway. I'm exhausted, but that's the only time I have to do my homework. More and more often, I fall asleep over my homework. When I finally get into bed, I have trouble sleeping; and when I get up in the morning, I have a terrible headache. It's getting harder and harder to do the things I have to do, but I feel I have to do them to get into a good college.

"Mom keeps telling me I'm under too much stress, and I should give up some of my activities before I really get sick. I don't think I can give anything up. I guess stress just goes with wanting to do a lot of different things."

Daniel is under a lot of stress, and he is experiencing several signs of stress. Continuous stress—stress that continues for a long period of time—can lead to physical symptoms much more serious than a headache in the morning. When there is a lot of stress in your life, and it goes on for a while, you need to make some changes. But before you can make any changes to reduce your level of stress, you need to be aware that you do have stress and recognize the symptoms. Once you acknowledge that there is a problem, then you can start making the changes that will help you cope with stress.

If you have physical problems associated with stress, discuss them with your parent, a teacher, a counselor, or a doctor. Don't be tempted to treat just the symptom—such as taking something to relieve a headache—without also making some changes in your lifestyle to relieve the stress. Stress may show up as a physical symptom, but there is always an emotional factor as well. First, you need to identify the stressor: What is causing your stress? Then you need to consider your reaction to the stressor: Are you making the stressor more serious than it needs to be?

Sometimes, just one change in your life can make a big difference. Doing one thing differently is a start. If Daniel volunteers only one day a week or one day a month at the animal hospital, it might relieve a lot of pressure.

Taking some small action can help to alleviate some of your stress. Simply phoning a friend to talk is a step in the right direction. When you come up with a good plan of action, stick to it, but stay flexible enough to try other ideas.

SELF-TALK

Talking to yourself and using your mind to cope with stress means setting goals, establishing priorities, getting organized, using problem-solving techniques, and taking action. You can develop a positive mental attitude, maintain your sense of humor, and stay in control while keeping everything in perspective. You can take responsibility for your own behavior and choose to act on your stress.

Be aware of your limitations, however. If a problem is beyond your control, you may need help from others. You might have to delay the resolution of a problem until you are able to handle it better. In that case, you need to accept the situation as it is, at least until a time when it can be resolved. Try to focus on what you do have control over. Do things in moderation; strive for excellence, not perfection. Forget about always winning.

When a situation makes you very angry or depressed, try to get away from it for a while so you can cool down and put it in perspective. You may need to set aside a problem until you can deal with it more effectively. Remember that a situation may be temporary, or may be more manageable when you take a break from thinking about it.

Have a "one day at a time" and "one problem at a time" attitude. While you are in school, don't worry about those stressors that affect you at home or at work. When you are at home, let go of the things in other parts of your life that are bothering you. Thinking about everything at once can make the problems seem overwhelming, and you may think that you can't handle any of them. Don't dwell on past mistakes, and don't just depend on tomorrow to be better. Plan for the future, but act for today.

THE POWER OF POSITIVE THINKING

Think positively. Be hopeful and realistically optimistic. Try to look at a stressful situation in a more positive way. "When my boss yelled at me for doing something wrong, I was ready to quit," says Mitch, sixteen. "I thought, who needs the stupid job, anyway! There was just too much stress. Then I realized that I like the work, and I need the money. I know I can do a better job if I want to, so I'm going to try. I concentrated on doing things better by being more careful, coming in on time, and things like that. Well, it worked. The boss was happy, so there was less stress. I even got a raise."

When you're "talking to yourself," make up a positive or optimistic phrase that you can repeat to help reduce negative thinking, such as, "I can handle anything." At the end of the day, think of something new and good that happened during the day. Don't allow negative thoughts to overwhelm the positive. Stay away from negative people and people who resort to violence or use drugs to avoid their problems.

Sixteen-year-old Christie knows the value of positive thinking. "I had an argument with my friend Alex on a Friday afternoon. I'm afraid I said some things I shouldn't have, and I may have hurt her feelings. I felt guilty and depressed, but I couldn't talk to Alex all weekend. All the negative thoughts kept building up in my head; it was giving me a headache and a stomachache. I knew that I had to try to think of something positive or I would be stressed out. So, I thought of all the good things I've said to Alex, and all the fun things we've done together.

"When I finally saw Alex on Monday, I had a positive attitude. I was able to smile and say 'hi' and really mean it. If I had let my stress build up, I may have been too angry, and who knows what I might have said. Instead, we worked things out, and we're still friends. I think it shows you've got to try to think positively."

Allow Yourself to Have Emotions

Having a positive attitude is one way of approaching stress and coping with it. However, your positive attitude must reflect your feelings. Holding in feelings and just trying to look happy without working through the cause of your stress can only lead to more stress. Whatever you feel is okay, including anger; there are no right or wrong feelings. It's how you express your emotions—whether in a positive or destructive way—that is important.

Develop or maintain a sense of humor. Laughing is an emotional release. The person who said "Laughter is the best medicine" wasn't joking! When you feel stressed, smile and say something nice to someone else. You'll both feel better. Do something that makes you smile or laugh; but don't laugh or joke about your serious concerns. You should take them seriously.

Crying can also help to relieve some stress, and may even prevent a headache or other symptoms. Holding in your emotions slows down the process of coping with stress. Crying helps clear your mind so coping can begin.

Avoid the three kinds of negative thinking that one counselor calls "mind traps": exaggeration ("That's the worst thing I could have done." "My friends will never speak to me again."); generalization ("I always do the wrong thing."); and negative self-talk ("Boy, am I stupid."). Remember that everyone goes through stressful times and makes mistakes. Your situation is a normal part of the maturing process.

SETTING GOALS

Coping with stress should be goal-driven. You need to ask yourself: What are my goals? How can I reach my goals in a positive way? Will my decisions create more or less stress in my life?

Setting goals includes establishing priorities and keeping things in perspective. Some stressful situations are very serious and may require professional counseling in order to be resolved. Other situations that may seem stressful for the moment are not threatening to your life or your lifestyle.

An important step in establishing goals is setting priorities. You can't do everything you want to do or have to do, and trying to do everything usually leads to a lot of stress. That is why you have to prioritize your activities; that is, put them in order of importance to you.

When you set priorities, you need to think about your values and your goals. There are some things you *must* do, such as go to school or to your job. There are things you *ought* to do: for instance, write Aunt Bessie a thank-you note or clean your room. There also are things you *want* to do: perhaps run on the track team or try out for the school play.

You can start by making a list of the tasks you have to do and want to do, with the most important ones first. Then do one task at a time, checking it off as it is completed. As you make your list, ask yourself, "Is this task necessary?"

You Can Say No

Give yourself permission to say *no* once in a while (but not all the time) to things you *ought* to do. When you feel pressured to do things you don't want to do, you are wasting both physical and emotional energy.

You can cope with stress by saying no to something that will add to your stress. "I was honored when our senior class president asked me to be the chairman of the prom committee," says Jeff. "I really had to think about it. I'm already involved in a lot of sports and activities in school, too many hard classes, and even a part time job. I finally had to say no, although that made me feel bad. I'm already stressed; adding one more thing would probably make me crazy."

When your stress is the result of a serious problem, such as the illness or death of a family member, you may have to think differently about the way you do things. You may need to postpone some decisions you are asked to make and some of the activities you are asked to take care of. This is the time when you have a right to say no to some requests.

ORGANIZING YOUR LIFE

Get organized, and you've taken one big step on the way to reducing stress. What does it take to get organized? Try getting up earlier and giving yourself more time in the morning. Lay out your school clothes the night before. Make your lunch the night before. Have your books, sports equipment, and other school things by the door. You can avoid some of the mad scramble to find everything in the morning and start your day on a less stressful note. With your family, organize some tasks such as meal planning and preparation and other household tasks, so the family can work together. In this way, one person won't have the stress of doing everything.

Write everything down that you need to do and remember. Make lists. Make up a time schedule that includes those things you *have* to do, such as school, your job, homework, and household chores; also allow some time for the things you *want* to do, such as shopping or watching television.

While you are setting goals, listing priorities, and writing schedules, be sure to include time to do something you like that will allow you to tune out your worries for a while. That's what sixteen-year-old Vanessa did when she tried out for the soccer team. Vanessa is one of the top students in her high school class, taking advanced classes in English, math, and science. She has won awards for her English essays. She is also a member of the student council.

"Everyone thought I was crazy to try out for soccer when I had so much studying and so many responsibilities," Vanessa says. "I think they understand now that I needed soccer so I could get away from all the pressures and stress. It really works. When I'm playing soccer, I can't worry about anything else. When I have to go back to studying I feel better about it. I also like being with people that I might not have met otherwise."

To help reduce stress, it is important to take time to do something you like, something that makes you feel comfortable, or something that makes you feel calm. You can choose from a variety of activities that will make you feel good and that don't involve a lot of planning, a lot of money, or a lot of thought.

An appropriate activity can be something as simple as eating a peanut butter and jelly sandwich, cleaning a closet, feeding the birds, or writing to a far-away friend. You can take a walk, read a mystery, take a bath, bake cookies, learn a new song, run a mile, start a collection, or volunteer and help someone who needs it. Do some kind of activity on a regular basis that is calming for you. Occasionally you might do something with your parent that is calming for you both.

Sophia says, "When I feel stressed, I sit down and play the piano." Juan finds another outlet for his stress: "I like to go to a soccer game and scream at our opponents." Whatever the activity, it is important that you work it into your schedule.

When a member of your family is ill or has died, you may feel reluctant to do something that makes you feel better. However, even in this situation, it is important to do something you enjoy to relieve some of the stress you feel. You actually need to take a break from worry and grieving.

THINK ABOUT YOUR PROBLEMS

Besides planning work and recreation, you can set aside a special time in your schedule for worrying, too. This way, worrying won't interfere with the rest of your life, adding stress. Just thinking about your problems may lead you to a plan of action or a solution. Try not to worry about things that are beyond your control, however.

If the source of your stress is the illness or death of a family member or friend, set aside time to think about that person and your good memories of his or her life. Write about your feelings in a journal. In that person's memory, do something you enjoy. Share your memories with others.

TECHNIQUES FOR PROBLEM-SOLVING

Another way that "talking to yourself" can help you cope with stress is through the use of problem-solving techniques. Sometimes stress comes from the feeling that you have no control over your problems. When you always rely on others to solve your problems, you lack control. However, when you work on solving your problems yourself, it gives you a sense that you can overcome the difficulty. It gives you a feeling of self-worth and boosts your self-esteem.

When you are under stress, or if you think a situation may begin to cause you stress, take a step back to understand the real problem and the best way to approach it. Size up the problem and consider the options to resolve it. Take time to think things through. Today is not the only day of your life. Think about alternatives, explore options, and look in new directions. You are putting yourself under pressure when you try to make immediate or impulsive decisions. Also, if you make a decision too quickly, you may realize later that you actually had other options that you did not take time to consider.

Use a step-by-step plan to solve problems and reduce stress. Here's one approach.

- **Identify the problem.** What is the problem causing the stress? Focus on the true problem.
- **Explore solutions to the problem.** Look at a variety of options for solving the problem. Be realistic; keep in mind your goals and values. Prioritize your solutions based on how realistic and effective you think they may be.
- **Try one of the options** and see if it helps solve your problem. First, try the solution you think is best. If it doesn't work, try another.

You need a variety of coping options. Different situations call for different approaches, and you need to be able to choose your strategy. When trying to cope with a stressful situation, you may be able to change the stressor by modifying or eliminating it. On the other hand, you may have to change your own routine or lifestyle to avoid the situation. You may have to change your thinking: The situation might seem less stressful if you look at it with a more positive attitude.

MAKE YOUR OWN DECISIONS

In order to avoid the stress that comes from peer pressure, you need to think for yourself. Decide if a situation is right for you without judging others. Your self-esteem will be boosted when you know you can make your own decisions.

"Some of my friends were putting a lot of pressure on me to do drugs with them," says sixteen-year-old Guy. "It was causing me a lot of stress, until I decided that drugs just did not fit into my plans for the future. I made a decision, and I feel good about it. The stress is gone, at least in that part of my life."

Making your own decisions is an important step in the maturing process. As you learn to evaluate situations and to react according to how you feel is best, you are discovering how to rely on yourself. You are developing inner strength that will be with you for the rest of your life. You will learn how to live with both good and bad decisions, and this experience will help you to make better choices in the future.

LOOKING TO RELIGIOUS FAITH

Some teens will tell you that the best stress relief comes through religion and prayer. Some teens, such as fifteen-year-old Cassie, grew up in a religious home. "Religion has always been a part of my life," Cassie says. "I won't say that I have no stress, but I think having faith sometimes helps. Getting ready for religious holidays can be really stressful, but you do get a secure feeling when you have all those family traditions."

Other teens are discovering religion for the first time, either because there was no religion in the home, or because they were not paying attention. "I started doing drugs when I was only thirteen," says Randy, who is now seventeen. "I think it was a response to stress, but I was as low as you could get and still be breathing. My parents finally got me into a rehab program. That's when I learned you don't have to carry the weight of the world all by yourself. There is someone else—a higher power, if you want to call it that—who can help. I'm not a very religious person, but I think religion has helped relieve a lot of my stress."

MENTAL IMAGING

Mental imaging can help you respond positively to stress. If you have to give a speech, sing a solo in the choir, try out for cheerleading, or interview for a job, you probably anticipate that you will have some stress. Along with your preparation and rehearsal, try a "mental rehearsal," too. Visualize your performance, but also visualize the stress that you will feel and the best way to respond to that stress. A "mental rehearsal" can give you added confidence. It can positively affect your performance as well as your physical responses to stress.

Mental images can help you relax. Neal likes to think of lying on the beach.

"Believe it or not, I like to do math problems in my head when I want to relax," says Della. "When you're doing math, you can't worry about anything else; and anyway, if I make a mistake, who's going to know?"

WRITING IT DOWN

Writing can also help to reduce stress. When you write about the stressors in your life, you can clarify what is causing your stress, and you may come up with some solutions. Writing essays or poems helps to release tension. "Writing about my problems helps me to feel better. No one has to read what I wrote and get mad at me," says Carlos, fifteen.

You can keep a journal and write something every day, or write only occasionally. Have a special notebook and pen for your writing. Write about the causes of your stress, but write about the nice things in your life, too. Just writing down your feelings and your worries is a way to relieve stress. If a family member or friend is ill or has died, write about that person and your good memories. Through writing, you can clarify your problems in your own mind. If you like to draw or paint, you can illustrate your feelings that way, or create pictures to go with your writing.

Fourteen-year-old Tess used writing to help her cope with stress. "When my little sister, Liza, was injured in a car accident, she was in the hospital for several weeks. Then she was allowed to come home in a body cast. Mom took care of her most of the time, but sometimes I had to stay home to help. I really got mixed-up feelings. I wanted to help my mother and be nice to my sister. But I also wanted to be with my friends and do things for myself. I didn't think it was fair. I got so upset about it that I started to feel sick.

"One day, when I was home and Liza was sleeping, I decided to write about my feelings. I wrote a little every day after that. Just writing down the things that I couldn't tell my mother or my friends helped me to feel better. I even wrote a story to tell Liza. She liked it, and that made me feel better about her and about myself."

Compile lists, too. When you have a decision to make, make a pro and con list: jot down everything in favor of a particular action, and everything against it. This will help you weigh the decision. When you feel you are making good decisions, it gives you a sense of control. That is a positive way to reduce your feelings of stress.

TALKING TO YOURSELF

Talking to yourself helps to relieve stress by clarifying your problems in your own mind; helping you establish goals, set priorities, and get organized; and creating a positive attitude. Often you can take charge of your problems and your life and work to resolve your own issues. Taking charge of your life also means taking responsibility for your own emotions. You do have a choice. You can bring your emotions under control.

Talking to yourself is good, but you are not the only person you need to talk to. Teens often feel they have to keep to themselves, but it is important to talk and to share with others: family members, friends, or counselors and other professionals.

Talk to yourself and others, take time to relax, and find the positive side of things. By keeping in touch with how you feel, you can give your mind what it needs to cope with a stressful situation.

CHAPTER 7

Help Yourself: Using Your Body to Cope with Stress

"**L**ast Monday, I was so angry with my coworker, I got really dizzy. I thought I was going to faint," says Brenda, seventeen. "I had to take a walk around the block to calm down."

"When I was the soloist with the school orchestra, I had indigestion for a week," says fifteen-year-old Anthony. "The funny thing is, that was the week *after* the concert!"

Sixteen-year-old Shamir says, "When I took the big math test, I was sweating, even though the room was cold. My muscles were so tight, I could hardly hold the pencil. I thought I had some weird disease, but I guess it was only stress."

PHYSICAL EFFECTS OF STRESS

The effects of stress show how your mind and your body work together. Stressful situations can lead to a variety of physical problems, including headaches, dizziness, stomachaches, rapid heartbeat, high blood pressure, tense muscles, and skin disorders. If you treat your body appropriately, you can reduce the effects of stress on your body.

Because stress can lower your body's resistance to disease, you are more susceptible to illness when you have stress. That's why it is so important to take good care of yourself by eating right, getting enough sleep, and exercising. When your daily routine is disrupted following a crisis or disaster, you need to get back to normal as soon as possible.

TAKING CARE OF YOURSELF

Eating right, getting exercise, and taking time to relax or have fun are always good ideas. These behaviors ensure that your body has what it needs to function properly. These practices can also help to reduce stress or even prevent it in the first place.

It may seem almost impossible to change your eating habits. If you like fast food or products with caffeine or sugar in them, such as soda, candy, or desserts, you may not want to give them up too quickly. In fact, you may think that eating food like this reduces your stress because it makes you feel better. However, these foods contain stimulants, which can add more stress to an existing problem. Reducing such foods can help to reduce stress. Eating food to reduce stress can lead to overeating, a serious symptom of stress.

It is important to get a good night's sleep. If you have trouble sleeping, or are sleeping too much, this may be a sign of stress. "I've got to get at least six hours of sleep a night in order to function in school the next day," says Michelle, sixteen. "I try to finish my homework before I go to bed or in the morning; but even if I don't, I'm better off when I get enough sleep. Otherwise, I develop a headache or I feel dizzy. I have a bad attitude with my friends and even my teachers, and you know that's not good. Everything just goes from bad to worse when I don't get enough sleep."

THE VALUE OF EXERCISE

Besides eating right and getting enough sleep, try to include some exercise in your daily routine. Take part in individual sports such as jogging, swimming, bike riding, or walking; or participate in team sports after school. Play basketball or baseball with friends in the neighborhood, or just throw around a Frisbee. Outdoor activities could also include mowing the lawn or gardening. You can do aerobics or yoga by yourself, with friends, or at your local park district or community center.

"My friends couldn't believe it when I went out for track, but it was the best thing I ever did," says Gina, seventeen. "I'm taking several advanced classes in school, so I'm getting a lot of pressure from my teachers and my parents. I got so stressed, I couldn't sleep at night, and I would get headaches all the time.

"To fit in time for practice, I had to adjust my schedule, and that wasn't easy. Still, when I get out on the track and I'm running or jumping, I forget all about the work and the pressures and my parents, too. Even though I have less time for studying, I can work more efficiently and get more done. I feel better about it, too. I can really cope with the pressure now.

"My friend Monica says the same thing. She's in the gymnastics program after school, and it helps her cope with the pressures at home since her parents separated."

When you are under stress, your body reacts with a "fight-or-flight" response, which involves increasing your heart rate, breathing rate, blood pressure, and muscle tension. Physical exercise helps to use some of that energy and reduce the symptoms. Exercise is good for you mentally and emotionally, as well as physically. It can increase your self-confidence and self-esteem, help you feel in control, and improve your outlook on life. It can help you to relax and temporarily get your mind off other stressors in your life.

Start your exercise program slowly and build from there, especially if you have never exercised regularly before. In the beginning, plan noncompetitive activities that you can do by yourself or with friends, such as running or bike riding. This way you can work at your own pace, increasing your activity each day. Talk to your doctor about possible limitations and also suggestions for the best type of exercise for you. Plan your exercise time into your daily schedule, so fitting it in won't cause more stress.

Doing household chores, or any task or activity that you are committed to doing well and completing, can help reduce stress. These activities can keep you from getting bored (which can be stressful); they can take your mind off other stressful problems temporarily; and they can boost your self-esteem by giving you a sense of accomplishment. Your parents may also be appreciative of your efforts.

BREATHING AND RELAXATION

When you engage in physical exercise, good breathing habits will increase your efficiency: you will use less energy while increasing the amount of exercise you do. Learning proper breathing techniques can help to reduce the symptoms of stress. If you are not breathing properly, less oxygen is going to your brain, and you can't function at full capacity. Deep, slow breathing can reduce the symptoms of stress by relaxing muscles and slowing the heart rate.

Deep, slow breathing is also one step in the relaxation process, another excellent method to help reduce stress and the symptoms of stress. There are a variety of relaxation methods that you can use, including progressive relaxation, breathing exercises, meditation, massage, and listening to quiet music. Just as stress has a usually negative effect on your body, relaxation can prompt positive physical changes. When you relax, your heartbeat and breathing may slow down, and there may even be a drop in blood pressure. Relaxation can help to reduce pain, including headaches and back pain, by reducing muscle tension.

The form of relaxing that you choose can be completely passive, such as simply lying down or sitting still and freeing your mind of distracting thoughts. Imagine something peaceful. "When I want to relax, I think about this picture I once saw in a magazine," says Risha, thirteen. "In the picture, someone was lying in a hammock, and the hammock was on a boat. It looked so relaxing. I know I'll never do anything like that; but when I want to relax, I think about how that must feel, and it helps."

With progressive relaxation, you progressively tense and then relax each area of the body. For example, you first tense and relax the muscles of the foot, then the calf, and then the thigh muscles, and so on. With this procedure, you concentrate on your body, learn to relax your muscles, and temporarily take your mind off your stress.

Relaxation may also come from just doing something you enjoy. Even when your stress is caused by a serious event, such as the illness of a family member, you need to occasionally take time out to do something that you like.

"When I try to relax by lying down or meditating, I feel even more anxious," says sixteen-year-old Afram. "I guess it makes me nervous to be doing nothing. But if I play jazz on the piano or listen to jazz, I really relax. I think jazz is the most relaxing music in the world."

Different people find different activities relaxing. In fact, what seems relaxing to one person may feel stressful to another. When a group was asked what they did to relax, answers included the following:

- Take a walk
- Swim
- Meditate
- Exercise
- Read
- Pray
- Play the plano
- Knit
- Breathe deeply
- Imagine a happy time
- Take a ten-minute nap

There are other techniques besides relaxation—including meditation, biofeedback, massage, and Restricted Environment Stimulus Therapy (R.E.S.T.)—that may reduce stress and the symptoms of stress. It is good to learn and use a combination of techniques.

MEDITATION

Through the use of meditation, you can reach a level of relaxation that is calming to your body and counters the negative effects of stress. To meditate, sit or lie down in a relaxed position, close your eyes, and concentrate on only one object or word, clearing your mind of other thoughts and distractions. Pay special attention to your breathing as you inhale and exhale. Your breathing and heart rate will slow down, and your blood pressure will be reduced.

BIOFEEDBACK

Biofeedback helps you understand and change the way stress affects your body. You select a bodily function which has been affected by stress that you would like to change or regulate, such as heart rate, blood pressure, skin temperature, or muscle tension. With the aid of electronic equipment, you monitor the function. You can learn to modify the function, and, using mental and physical techniques such as imaging or proper breathing, you can reduce your pulse rate, blood pressure, tension headaches, or other stress symptoms.

"My muscles were getting so tense during gymnastics practice, I wasn't doing anything right," says Justin, fifteen. "Every time I made a mistake, it caused me more stress, so things kept getting worse. I think my gymnastics coach was afraid I might get hurt, so he suggested that I try biofeedback.

"The first time I tried biofeedback, I felt like I was in one of those old science fiction movies. They attached wires to my muscles and then to a machine that monitored the muscle tension. When my muscles were tense, the machine beeped; the more tension, the more beeping.

Then, they taught me how to relax the muscles, so there was less beeping. After a while, I was able to recognize what muscles were tense and relax them even without the machine. Now I can relax before gymnastics practice and before a competition. I'm doing much better, and I have much less stress."

OTHER ACTIVITIES FOR REDUCING STRESS

Massage can help to lower heart rate and blood pressure, improve circulation, and relax tense muscles. Massage will help you feel better psychologically. Through massage, you become more aware of your body and when it is experiencing the symptoms of stress, so that you can work to eliminate some of the sources of stress.

Restricted Environment Stimulus Therapy (R.E.S.T.) is a form of sensory deprivation. Participants float in a pool or lie on a bed in a stimulus-free environment, with no light or sound. The air or water is the same temperature as the human body. Such an environment does reduce some of the effects of stress.

Taking care of a pet or a garden can often reduce your levels of stress and the symptoms of stress. "My dog, Ginger, is just a mutt we got at the Humane Society, but she's the best thing in my life right now," says fourteen-year-old Stacey. "When I come home from a stressful day at school—if a teacher has made me really angry, or I've had a fight with a friend—I know Ginger will be there to greet me. Ginger makes me feel so important, I can forget about my problems for a little while. When I need to talk to someone, Ginger is the one who is sure to listen; and she always seems to agree with me, too!"

"My garden is my stress reducer," says Quinn, thirteen. "Even though we live in the city where nothing seems to grow, I've got this big wooden tub on our back porch filled with petunias and marigolds. The seeds are pretty inexpensive. I started the flowers from scratch inside the house. It makes me feel good that I have accomplished something worthwhile. Best of all, when I feel angry or frustrated, all I have to do is pull a couple of weeds, and I get relief!"

Take a break from your daily routine. Relax, have fun, and do something you like once in a while. Participate in a sport; paint a picture; listen to music; play an instrument; or do whatever makes you feel relaxed and happy.

Eighteen-year-old Linda likes to go to dance class after work. "Answering the phone all day, doing secretarial work, and putting things together for the boss, I sometimes feel like I'm running the whole office," Linda says. "My muscles tighten up and I'm sure my blood pressure goes up, too. So, when I get to dance class, all I have to think about is stretching out those muscles and moving to the music. It's a great stress fighter."

Charles, sixteen, likes photography. "My dad taught me photography. He was a professional photographer, at least until he got sick. I like to photograph people in the neighborhood. I know Dad likes to see the pictures, and I'm glad I have something to share with him.

"When Dad first got sick, I was afraid even to talk to him. It was very upsetting and stressful to me. I sometimes got sick to my stomach. Now that I'm sharing my interest with him, it's better. Photography also gives me time by myself to do something I like, and that helps with the stress. It makes me hopeful, too; maybe Dad will recover and we can work on photography together."

VOLUNTEERING

You can help yourself when you help others. Be a volunteer in your community—at the community center, with the park district, or at your local hospital, for example. Volunteer work has many advantages. It gives you a chance to think about something other than the events that are causing you stress; it builds your self-esteem because you are helping people in need and your community; and it can keep you from getting bored. When you volunteer, you meet new and interesting people and make new friends. You can learn new things.

Volunteer work can have a more practical side, as it did for fifteen-year-old Jay. "I never thought much about plants and flowers, except when we had a biology assignment," Jay says. "Then the volunteer director at the community center told me that they needed people to plant flowers around the high school. I decided to sign up just to get away from home on the weekends. That's when my parents seem to do the most fighting, and it's really causing me a lot of stress.

"I had to go to the plant nursery to pick up the plants. When I was there, I learned that there's a lot more to flowers than just something for Mom on Mother's Day. They are trying to grow healthy plants without using chemicals that are bad for the environment. I got so interested in the work, I started volunteering with the park district twice a month. I'm now planning to go into conservation or forestry after I finish high school. By the way, volunteering and doing something that interests me really did cut down on the amount of stress I feel. I don't get the bad headaches I used to get when I had to listen to Mom and Dad fight."

There are many ways to help yourself mentally and physically. Along with helping yourself, you may turn to others for help, too. Friends and family members, professional counselors, support groups and organizations are there to help when you are experiencing stress and the effects of stress. It's all right to ask for help.

CHAPTER 8

Talking to Friends and Family

"**W**hen the hurricane warnings went up, I was scared," says fourteen-year-old Grant. "I didn't want anyone to know how I felt, even though it was giving me a headache and my heart was racing. Mom said we had to go to higher ground because of my younger brother and sister, so I agreed. I was glad the family could stay together, even though we weren't in our house.

"The Red Cross worker got some families together to talk. I didn't want to talk, even though she said it would be a good thing. I listened to the other families, and I realized that everyone felt pretty much like I did, even this kid from school who was older than me. Some of the families had gone through other bad hurricanes, and they survived. I learned that, although the hurricane was bad, it wasn't the end of the world, and we would get back to normal some day.

"I finally said a few things about how I felt. I even suggested how we could entertain the younger kids so they wouldn't be so frightened, and everyone liked my idea. It's hard to believe, but I really did feel better after that. Like the Red Cross worker said, it was good to let my feelings out instead of bottling them up inside."

EXPRESSING EMOTIONS

When you are striving to cope with stress, two factors are important: you need warm and supportive relationships with family and friends, and you need to talk. However, when you are under stress, whether it's from a disaster or other problem, you may not want to talk to anyone or be with anyone. You need to recognize the benefits of talking to family and friends.

Just expressing feelings helps to reduce stress. Through talking, you learn that you are not alone, that you don't have to solve every problem by yourself. You discover that others have faced similar problems and survived. You can compare with others your responses to a stressful situation and know that you're not abnormal. Talking with others is also a positive action; you are reaching out to others rather than withdrawing.

Ideally, when you have stress, your home is the place where you can talk and where you find emotional support and encouragement. If you cannot talk to your parent or to an older sister or brother, try talking to a teacher, counselor, clergyperson, neighbor, or another relative. Share your worries with someone you trust and respect.

Spend Time with Family

During times of stress, you should be able to rely on your family and friends for emotional support. In fact, the caring and understanding of others can help reduce stress. People who care about you can help bring a sense of comfort and trust into your life. Uncertainty, lack of control, and change create stress in your life. Those who give you support offer you predictable behavior and shared values. This can help reduce some of the stress or even prevent it in the first place.

When you seek the support of those who care for you, or when you are offering your support to others, you need to communicate. By talking to others, you share your feelings and you learn about the feelings of others. Don't assume you know what other people are thinking, and don't assume they know how you feel unless you tell them.

Take time to talk with your parents and other family members each day. Schedule a regular time for talking— such as before bed or after dinner—and stick to it as much as possible. Keep the television and other distractions off while you talk.

Besides talking with one of your parents—or instead of talking, if that is a problem—try doing some activity together. Plan something you both like, such as going to a movie and then eating out afterward. You can walk, ride bikes, or do some other physical exercise together. This may open the lines of communication, and later you will be able to talk to your parent about more serious problems. Sharing an activity with your parent may help to reduce some of the stress you and your parent are feeling.

Talk to Someone You Trust

There are times when you may want to turn to an adult for information and support. However, you may feel, as many teenagers do, that you cannot talk to your parents. You may feel too embarrassed, or think your parents will not listen or will criticize too quickly. Often a parent is unavailable, because he or she is working outside the home or simply does not want to communicate. You should be able to talk to someone outside the family. You can turn to other adults such as a teacher, school counselor, member of the clergy, a neighbor, adult friend, or the parent of a friend.

To sixteen-year-old Philip, it seemed as if he had never been able to talk to his father. Philip was having problems with some friends at school. The longer these problems went unresolved, the worse they got and the more stress Philip felt. Philip needed to discuss the situation with someone.

Every time Philip went to his friend Gary's house, Gary's dad was there. His dad had a home office. Occasionally, when Philip and Gary would go into the kitchen for a snack, Gary's dad would join them, and Philip would start talking to him. "I can't talk to my own dad like I can talk to yours," Philip told Gary.

"That's weird," Gary replied. "I think it's easier to talk to *your* dad." After a few conversations with Gary's dad, Philip was encouraged to try to talk to his own father about some of the problems that were causing him stress.

Having people near you who care about you and who will listen to you is an important factor in reducing or avoiding stress. When you are under stress, it is a good idea to share your feelings with someone, whether those feelings are positive or negative. Just discussing with a parent, relative, friend, or neighbor how you feel can help to reduce the burden and let you know that you are not alone.

Just by talking, you can:

- **Let off steam.** Before you can attack a problem, you need to calm down so you can think clearly.
- **Clarify problems.** Talking can sometimes help you focus on a problem. You can make choices and decisions. It can give you hope and ideas for action to help solve some of your problems.
- **Share ideas.** The person you are talking with may have some new ideas for you. He can listen to your thoughts and opinions and add to them or modify them. While talking, you may come up with some new solutions in your own mind.
- **Get encouragement.** Another person can give you comfort and support and increase your self-esteem.
- **Reduce feelings of being alone or helpless.** You no longer have to feel as if you are dealing with your problems all by yourself. You are not alone.
- **Put things in perspective.** Another person's point of view and experience may help you see your problems, and the stress that goes with them, in a different light.

SEEK SOLUTIONS

When you talk to a friend or with your family, discuss specific problems. Discuss alternatives to each problem and try to find realistic goals and solutions. Others should offer their support and not simply tell you what to do. Good communication should help you make your own decisions, not just give you advice.

Communicating in the right way can help you and your parents solve problems, negotiate, compromise, and settle differences. You want certain things from your parents, such as independence and moral and financial support.

Your parents want things from you, such as appropriate behavior and success in school. Through communication and compromise, you and your parents can reduce the stress that these conflicting ideas might cause.

Discuss with your parents how you might handle a stressful situation. Discuss different solutions and possible results. If your parents' expectations and demands are the source of your stress, you can try making a contract with your parents for change. If you improve your behavior, then your parents will reduce their demands or expectations of you. For example, you might agree: "I'll practice the piano for half an hour every day and you'll stop asking me about it." Try to compromise and reach a balance, some middle ground, where neither you nor your parents feel you are compromising your standards.

You and your parents should establish some ground rules for your behavior at home. How will you handle your anger and your disagreements? Discuss the consequences of not following the rules. Know ahead of time what to expect if you don't keep up your end of the contract.

COMMUNICATION SKILLS

Brush up on your communication skills. That includes not only expressing how you feel, but also listening to the other person. Don't think up an answer while the other person is speaking; let her finish. Look for clues to her feelings in her behavior, tone of voice, and facial expression: Is she nervous, shy, angry, or sad? Express your own feelings about a situation without blaming others for the problem. Keep your sense of humor.

At the beginning of your discussion, try to get all the information you need by using active listening skills. Try to understand what the person is saying and thinking, not just from her words, but from her facial expressions and "body language." In your own words, repeat what the person has said so you know you understand correctly.

Don't drag up old arguments or old problems (some people call that "garbage dumping"). Remember the times you have resolved conflicts successfully. Don't be afraid to negotiate and compromise. Some issues can be negotiated, such as whether you need a haircut or whether you need to clean your room. Other issues cannot be negotiated, such as going to school.

Communication can reduce stress and also help avoid some stressful situations. You should speak up to express your feelings, but be sure to cool down first. Think about the problem and clarify your position; be specific. Talk about your own feelings. Don't blame someone else for the problem. Don't analyze someone else's feelings, ridicule him, or tell him how he should think or feel. Everyone is responsible for his or her own behavior. Be tolerant of other people's differences.

The following steps will help you and your parents solve problems and reduce stress:

- **Discuss** one problem at a time. Be sure you and your parents are clear about the exact problem that you are discussing.
- Everyone involved in the discussion should **offer ideas** on ways of handling the problem.
- After all the ideas have been presented, each person may give his or her **opinion** of each one. **Eliminate** the options that have too many negatives or just won't work.
- From the alternatives that are left, **choose** the one you will try or, if necessary, create more.
- **Try** out the chosen solution. Give it time.

- **Analyze** whether the solution worked the way you expected it to. What was good about it and what was not? Then you can decide to continue with the solution as it is, modify it, or choose to try something different.

"Everybody tells you to discuss your problems with your parents. Well, we don't exactly discuss things in my house; it's more like an argument or a real fight, if you want to know the truth," says fourteen-year-old Leon. "At least my dad hasn't thrown me out of the house yet. My dad's strict rules are giving me a lot of stress. When he yells at me, it adds to the stress.

"Most of the time it's about my curfew. My dad wants me home even before the city curfew. That's not fair, because all my friends get to stay out at least until then. My dad always brings up the one night I came in late. That was a year ago, but he's still throwing it in my face, and usually just as I'm going out the door. The situation got so bad, I started to get stomachaches just thinking about it. I thought maybe I should just sneak out before Dad could yell at me, but that only made me feel worse.

"When I complained to my teacher, he said my dad and I should try discussing this problem when we're both calm, and not just as I'm going out. He said I might be able to negotiate something. I would never have believed my dad would do that, but he did. Maybe he was getting tired of yelling.

"When we discussed it, Dad listened to my reasons for wanting to be with my friends, and I listened to why he was worried about me being out late in our neighborhood, which isn't the safest in the world. We talked about ways to compromise, and we finally worked it out. Dad said I could slowly work up to the city curfew, as long as I always came in on time. He also said that the first time I came home late, my curfew would be put back even earlier than before. I agreed to that, and you can bet I haven't been late since!"

Pick a Good Time to Talk

Calm down before communicating. Don't talk over a problem when either you or your parents, or all of you, are already angry. You can't have a meaningful discussion when you feel so stressed that you are ready to explode. Don't just blurt out your complaint or criticism. Make an appointment for a later time, when you and your parents are ready to talk and listen. You might need to be by yourself for a while until you calm down.

Talking Leads to Understanding

Talking and listening help you and others understand each other's feelings. You can share and exchange feelings as well as ideas for solving problems. When you share problems, you feel better knowing you are not alone.

If you think that you are being asked to do too much at home—such as household chores and child care—and it is causing stress, you and your family need to communicate and negotiate. You can work together to reduce some of these tasks. Plan with your family how you can share some of your responsibilities at home, change them, or eliminate them altogether.

Of course, you can talk with people your age too. Talking to friends is probably what is most comfortable for you. Although another teen may not have the knowledge or experience of an adult, he or she can care and help, especially when the stressful situation involves another friend or a teenage brother or sister.

COPING WITH A FAMILY ILLNESS OR DEATH

If a crisis such as a serious accident, illness or death of a family member, a divorce, or the sudden unemployment of a parent is causing you stress, you must deal with the problem as well as the stress it causes. Your parents may be hurting or grieving, but they can help you, too. You should be kept informed about the status of the ill or injured person, or the cause of death. You should be included in events such as memorial services, and even help with some decisions. Know that it is all right to grieve or worry. It's okay for *anyone* to cry. Holding in these emotions and not expressing them can lead to serious physical and emotional symptoms of stress.

If your stress is the result of trying to cope with the serious illness or death of a parent, brother, sister, or friend, some special measures need to be followed. You will want to know what's going on, and you have a right to be told by your parents. Parents may be reluctant to tell you the truth because they are afraid it will frighten you. However, it can only add to your stress if you suspect that something is wrong, but your parent denies it or gives you inadequate information. You will probably want to know the details of exactly what the problem is (for instance, if a parent is dying of cancer), how it will affect the person with the disease, how it will affect you, and what is going to happen in the future.

After you are given the right information about the illness affecting your parent or brother or sister, you may want to take part in his or her care, helping to reduce your own stress as well as bring some happiness to the patient. At home—or in the hospital if regulations permit—you can read to the patient, decorate the room with pictures, or do something special that would bring a smile to the patient.

When Rosa's little sister, Carlita, was very ill following open-heart surgery, sixteen-year-old Rosa and her fourteen-year-old brother Luis were told all about the problem as well as Carlita's chances for recovery. Rosa was worried about Carlita, so worried that she couldn't sleep and seemed to have a constant headache. When Carlita was out of intensive care, the hospital allowed Rosa to come and read to Carlita. Rosa also brought pictures and made little ornaments to hang near Carlita's bed. Doing these things made Rosa feel better; her headache disappeared, and she was able to sleep at night. Rosa knew it made Carlita feel better, too, even though Carlita sometimes fell asleep before the end of the story.

Luis contributed in his own way by acting like a clown, making faces and bumping into things. Carlita laughed and called it "funny stuff."

When Carlita came home from the hospital, Rosa and Luis welcomed her. Now the family was faced with new stress because Carlita still required care at home. Once again, the family got together and talked, planned, and compromised. Carlita would receive the care she needed, and Rosa and Luis would still have time for school, activities, and getting together with friends.

With some illnesses or accidents, you realize that the family member will not recover. When a parent or brother or sister is dying, you need to make the most of the time left together. Even if you have never been close to this parent or brother or sister, doing little things for him or her is more important than ever to them and for your own peace of mind.

A teen can do many things to help in a household when a family member is ill or dying. However, a teen should never be expected to take the role of a parent. Instead, try to arrange for another adult—such as a relative, neighbor, or friend—to help with driving and chores, keeping the school informed, and communicating with people outside the family.

Following the death of a family member or close friend, it may take time before the family will be able to talk together. How long it takes to get to this point will differ with each member of the family. The family will need to talk, however, to share memories and feelings, to make decisions, or to plan a memorial service, event, or fund in memory of the family member who has died.

If death or illness affects your family, it is a time when you can ask others—such as a family friend, cousin, aunt or uncle, or neighbor—for assistance. When a family is grieving, people will offer to help, and it is all right to accept that offer. On the other hand, you may want to do something to help others, such as caring for a younger family member. Death or illness is out of your control, and that can cause stress. Helping others can help you feel more in control, which can help to reduce your stress.

COPING WITH GUILT

Guilt is another stressful emotion that you should work out by talking with others. You need to talk to an adult who understands your feelings, as fifteen-year-old Andrew did. "When my little brother Chris got hit by a car,

I decided it was my fault," Andrew says. "I sometimes walked with him to the park on Saturday mornings, because Mom had to work. I didn't want to walk with him that day, so I stopped to talk to some friends, and that's when the accident happened. I was so upset about it, I really got sick. I couldn't eat; I couldn't sleep; I even got a skin rash.

"I'm thankful now that Aunt Joan was around. I didn't want to talk to anyone, but she finally convinced me to talk to her. She's been a teacher, and she knew other kids who felt the same way after a brother or sister had been hurt. Just talking to Aunt Joan helped me feel a little bit better. I finally felt good enough to go and talk with the school counselor, who helped me even more."

You may also experience feelings of guilt when your parents divorce. Again, talking with others can help reduce the stress. You need to talk to your parents in order to understand why they divorced. Even though they are going through a tough time, they are still there for you.

"I'm glad I could talk to my older sister about our parents' divorce. She seems to understand it better than I do," says thirteen-year-old Tanya. "My sister sometimes ignores me, but this time she really listened and made me feel better."

"My mom and I are talking more now. I actually feel closer to her now than I did before she and Dad were divorced," says Maurice, fifteen.

Sixteen-year-old Gordie says, "When my parents decided to get a divorce, it was really stressful for me. I thought it was my fault, because I didn't live up to their expectations, or something like that. I started getting terrible stomachaches. After my dad moved out, there was less fighting, but I still felt stressed.

"I guess my parents were stressed, too, because it took some time before I could really talk to them. I started to see my dad more often than before the divorce, because now he wanted to be with me. Both my parents told me I wasn't to blame for the divorce. In fact they tried to stay together for my sake, but it just didn't work out."

"When my parents got a divorce, it was bad enough," says fourteen-year-old Ronna. "But, when my Mom said she had to go back to work, just to have enough money for food and rent, I was devastated. I was being abandoned! I was so upset, I felt dizzy, and I had a constant headache.

"Mom could see that I was upset and that this was causing a lot of stress. She said we should talk about the situation and my feelings. I didn't want to do that; it sounded pretty dumb, but Mom insisted. So, finally, Mom and I and my ten-year-old brother Ricky sat down together and talked about what Ricky would do after school, and how I would be able to keep up with all my activities. I'm really not home that much when Mom is working anyway. We worked out a schedule of what needed to be done around the house and who would do it. That helped me to organize my own life better. I always thought Ricky was a spoiled brat, but he actually started doing work around the house, as much as he could.

"I began to feel like I had less stress than before the divorce when Mom and Dad were always fighting. So out of a bad situation we managed to learn some good things, and it was mostly because we talked and worked things out."

Even if your parents have divorced, you should try to keep your life as normal as possible in order to reduce stress. The same is true following a disaster; you should also strive for normalcy.

DEALING WITH A DISASTER

Your family can work together as a unit to prepare for, go through, and recover from a disaster. Following a disaster, family ties may be strengthened as you discover that it is more important to preserve close relationships than material possessions. Talk with your family and friends about what has been lost. Talk with other families; share your feelings and your grief.

It is also important to talk with the mental health workers who will probably come to help during a disaster. Discuss the facts of the situation, but also discuss your fears and other feelings. Try to get back to normal as soon as possible, or at least carry out some of the tasks you normally do.

When you are going through a crisis or a disaster, you experience a great deal of stress. To relieve some of that stress, try to find something good in a bad situation. Sometimes a bad situation, such as a serious illness or a natural disaster, will pull together a family that was never close before. Many people who go through a tough time change their whole attitude about life and set new goals.

When you are under stress, you need to talk to others, and you need to be with other people who are supportive and encouraging. However, if you think that talking with family and friends is not helping, you may need to go a step further and speak with a professional counselor or join a support group.

CHAPTER 9

Talking to Counselors and Support Groups

t was two o'clock in the morning, and seventeen-year-old Sandra had been sitting on the edge of her bed for almost two hours. She should have been relieved now that exam week was over, but the stress of the past week had left her numb. Sandra felt cold and had a headache; her muscles were tight, and she felt nauseated. She may have said she was coming down with the flu, but she knew it was stress.

Sandra couldn't talk to her parents or her friends. Most of her friends, including her on-again-off-again boyfriend, did not phone all week because they were studying, too. She was sure that she had not done well on her exams, which might hurt her chances of going to college. Now, she wasn't so sure she even wanted to go to college. What was she going to do with the rest of her life?

Sandra was sad, angry, and frustrated. She wanted to throw something, break something, or just run away. Two months before, she would have done those things, destroying property and hurting others or herself. Tonight Sandra did not do anything destructive. Instead, she picked up the phone and called Kurt, the counselor from the social services center who had been helping her for the last few months.

When Kurt got the call from Sandra, he knew it had taken courage for her to phone. Her phone call meant she needed help in controlling her reactions to her stressful feelings. After talking for a while, Kurt was able to convey the message to Sandra that she could handle her feelings. Kurt knew that, with his help, Sandra was learning a constructive way of managing her stress. She could make the right decisions now, and she could overcome the wrong choices and actions she had followed in the past.

Kurt is one of the many professional people who can help teenagers cope with stress and manage their emotional and physical reactions to stress. These professionals—including physicians, nurses, clergy, counselors, social workers, and therapists—have special knowledge to help you solve specific problems. They work with individuals, groups, families, children, adolescents, and adults.

THERAPISTS

You may be reluctant to see a counselor or therapist about stress-related problems. Surveys show that only about 25 percent of teenagers consider going to a counselor for help with stressful problems. Often teens have a negative view of most counselors, teachers, and school officials. Like most teens, you may just try to cope on your own. However, keeping your feelings to yourself can increase stress and emotional problems. It is important for you to share feelings with others, whether they are friends, family, or professional counselors.

"I was so stressed by my parents' divorce, I was ready to try getting stoned to feel better," says Zack, fourteen. "The school counselor could tell things were getting out of control, so he referred me to a therapist. Wait, I thought, I'm not crazy, even if I'm acting a little strange. I found out that a therapist can help normal people who have problems they can't work out by themselves. The therapist helped me to understand my problems and myself. He helped my mom, too, because she was stressed out after the divorce."

A therapist or other counselor can help you learn the skills you need to cope with stress: setting goals, problem-solving, anger management, dealing with conflict, and handling change. You can examine the conflicts in your life, build self-esteem, and learn stress management. In family therapy, you can learn to share feelings and learn to communicate. With the help of a therapist, the whole family can learn coping skills.

Sometimes you can help yourself just by talking to friends or family, starting an exercise program, or working on a hobby. How do you know when you should look for professional help? Therapist Greg Newman suggests that whenever you think you might need professional help, that is the time to get it. Be aware of the symptoms of stress, but "don't wait for some special signal," Newman says. When your parents see signs of stress, they should speak with your teachers or school counselors.

After a death, a divorce, or other crisis or disaster, it takes a long time to return to what you would consider normal feelings and a normal life. If you think you are hanging onto anger, fear, or other stressful feelings for too long, it is time to seek professional help. You should give yourself time to solve your problem on your own, but set a deadline. If the situation doesn't improve by the deadline, get in touch with a counselor. You will probably be able to sense when your parents are too caught up in their own problems to really focus on your stress and give you the help you need. Counseling can be helpful when your family members are busy with their own concerns.

If you occasionally experience a few symptoms of stress that are not too serious, it is probably just a normal response to everyday problems. However, if you, your parents, or your teacher are aware of many symptoms, occurring often or to a serious degree, it is important to get professional help. Consider seeing a physician first to find the source of a physical problem, whether it seems to be stress-related or not. Don't make your own diagnosis.

It is normal to be sad, anxious, or overwhelmed once in a while, but continuous, severe, or debilitating sadness or anxiety that keeps you from living a normal life may be a sign of depression. You and your parents should be aware of these signs. When they occur, it's important to get medical help without delay.

If stress is causing you to consider some extreme solution to your problem, such as turning to drugs or alcohol, running away, or even attempting suicide, a crisis hot line can provide emergency help. "We don't want anyone to get hurt or to hurt themselves. That is where the crisis hot line really helps," says Greg Newman.

Many hospitals provide outpatient counseling, even in an emergency. As an outpatient, you do not check into the hospital as a patient. Sometimes, teens using alcohol or drugs are brought in by their parents or police. "A teen may walk in feeling suicidal, and we can give him immediate attention," one social worker says. Most cities have crisis lines where people may call trained counselors for immediate counseling.

FINDING A COUNSELOR

To find a counselor or therapist, start with your school counselor. Many schools provide the service of counselors free to students. Be sure to inform the school—your teacher, principal or counselor—when there is a crisis at home, such as the serious illness or death of a family member, a divorce, or a parent losing a job.

Your school may also provide health services that not only encourage good health practices, but also reduce stress by answering questions on contraception, sexually transmitted diseases, date rape prevention, and suicide prevention. Your school may be working to prevent or reduce stress among students by teaching conflict resolution and violence prevention. Find out what free services you can get at your school or in the community.

If your school counselor thinks you need more help than he or she can provide, he or she may refer you to outside sources—a social worker or psychologist—for further counseling. You can also get a referral from a friend, your doctor, a member of the clergy, or your local hospital or mental health center. You should like your counselor and feel comfortable working with him or her; otherwise, switch to someone else. A good counselor can help you as an individual, and may also help your family learn to communicate and work together.

A social worker who counsels teens with drug- or alcohol-related problems suggests that parents need to get into counseling, too. When parent and teenager can't talk together, they can start their counseling separately.

The aim is that eventually they will come together for counseling and communication.

Many counselors and therapists use a mind-body approach to deal with a patient's stress problems. They give equal attention to a person's mind, body, and spirit. Because stress affects you emotionally and physically, you may find this an effective approach.

Most therapists will concentrate on one problem area at a time, starting with the situations that require the most problem solving. The goal is to reinforce appropriate behavior and minimize inappropriate behavior.

OTHER RESOURCES FOR HELP

Besides school counselors and private-practice therapists, there are many resources in the community that can offer you professional help with stress-related problems. There are crisis hot lines in every city that you can phone anonymously for information and advice. A local mental health or social service center may offer outpatient programs for drug addiction or eating disorders. Police often employ social workers or youth workers to counsel teens who may have been locked out of their homes, who are running away, or who are involved with other police-related problems.

RESPONDING TO A CRISIS

Following a crisis or disaster, you may feel like things will never be normal again. You may even think that it is not right to try to get back to a normal situation. However, a counselor who works with disaster victims recommends going back to your normal routine as soon as possible. Be good to yourself. Eat right and get exercise.

You should talk to a counselor soon after the crisis or disaster—away from parents and brothers and sisters, if possible—to discuss your feelings. The longer you wait to talk to a counselor, the more difficult it may be. You don't want to put a shell around yourself, hold in your feelings, or brush problems aside by saying, "Everything is okay." This will only increase your stress.

Try to return to regular activities with friends. This is especially important after your family experiences a crisis such as a fire, when community institutions such as schools, churches and community centers are still intact and ready to help. Getting back to regular activities can also take place after a large-scale disaster, such as a hurricane, but it does take longer because the whole community may be struggling to return to normalcy.

TURNING TO YOUR COMMUNITY

Whether your stress is related to a disaster, or comes from the pressures of everyday life, many organizations and support groups in the community can help you directly or indirectly with those problems. Religious organizations, youth groups, civic groups, and scouts may have a support group or social worker to help with stressful situations, or may offer activities to help you release stress. You can join or form neighborhood groups that provide mediation programs to settle conflicts without aggression.

Helping Yourself by Helping Others

Sixteen-year-old Lars likes to talk about some of the activities offered at his community center. "They have a volunteer bureau, so kids who are bored can become volunteers," Lars says. "This was great for me. Last year, school seemed pointless. I started hanging out with some of the kids who were on drugs, my grades were slipping, and I was thinking about dropping out. I guess deep down it was really bothering me, because I had this constant headache and stomachache. I never slept well at all.

"The social worker at the community center recommended that I become a volunteer tutor for the little kids who come into the center after school. You would think that adding a job like that might cause even more stress for me, but it didn't. Helping those kids made me feel much better about myself. It also forced me to be better organized. Now I get my own homework done and my grades are better. I also don't get those headaches and stomachaches anymore. I sleep like a rock, especially on days when I tutor. I hope I can get a job helping out with the community day camp next summer, because then you get paid."

When you care for others, not just when others care for you, it can help you resist stress. Teens who volunteer are often able to build self-esteem and have a feeling of community, two factors that help reduce stress.

The same is true following a disaster such as a flood or hurricane. You can join the many volunteers at churches, schools, youth groups, and sports clubs who work together at this time of crisis. You can be a part of the network. You can keep busy at a shelter, caring for younger or older people, or you can do physical work such as filling sandbags.

COMMUNITY RESOURCES

Your local police may have programs that deal with the causes or the results of stress. Stealing, using drugs and alcohol, running away, vandalism, and violent behavior can be the causes of stress or responses to stress. If you are involved in any of these activities, you will probably be involved with the police, and the police may refer you to a counselor.

Work together with your parents, neighbors, and the police to reduce crime and violence, which are major sources of stress. Begin in your own home by turning off violent television shows. Join a neighborhood watch group or form one of your own to work with the police in eliminating drug houses and other criminal elements in your neighborhood.

Hospitals and Health Clinics

If your parent or a brother or sister is hospitalized for a serious illness, you can often find help for your stress right there in the hospital. Most hospitals have social workers who can help families deal with stressful problems. Hospital social workers can assist with both the emotional issues and the practical problems of managing a household before and after a patient returns home.

When worries about pregnancy, birth control, and safe sex are causing stress, you can find help in a community health clinic, just as sixteen-year-old Sharone did. Sharone was so worried about getting pregnant or getting AIDS and other sexually transmitted diseases that it was causing her stress. Sometimes she had headaches, stomachaches, and dizziness. This made Sharone worry even more; did her symptoms mean she really was sick or pregnant? Sharone was afraid to talk to her parents about her problems; she was sure they would not understand. They didn't approve of sex before marriage.

Sharone talked to her friend, Mei, who suggested that Sharone go to a local health clinic set up especially for young women. "For a small fee, you can get an exam, and they will test for infection and disease," Mei explained. "It's confidential. They won't tell your parents or anyone else."

It took a while for Sharone to get up the courage to make an appointment at the clinic. The first time she went, she was part of a small chat group that discussed pregnancy, birth control, and sexually transmitted diseases. Just talking to the other girls and discovering that they had similar worries made Sharone feel better. Finding out after her pelvic exam that she had no physical problems also reduced Sharone's stress symptoms.

Sharone now knew that she could always go to the clinic to discuss problems with the counselor. Sharone paid for the clinical visits with money she earned at her after-school job. This gave her a feeling of responsibility and control of her own life, something that also helped to reduce her stress. "It's not easy, but it's something I'm doing for myself," Sharone told Mei.

Many hospitals offer inpatient and outpatient programs for teens with behavioral problems or mental health problems that cause stress or that are the result of stress. Often a special program of individual, family, and group therapy is supervised by a team of professionals that includes medical doctors, psychologists, therapists, teachers, and social workers. Inpatient programs may be followed by outpatient counseling after school.

Religious Organizations

Religious institutions often provide a variety of programs, such as support groups and counseling, that can help teens reduce the stress in their lives. Religious observance itself may help reduce stress. Some therapists, even those not directly connected with a religious institution, incorporate a spiritual side to counseling. "It helps us to explain and live with our problems," one therapist says.

STRESS MANAGEMENT PROGRAM

You may need a special stress management program when your family or home situation is the source of your stress. If your family has experienced divorce, abuse, the illness or death of a family member, if your parent is having a problem dealing with his or her own stress, or if you live in an area subject to violence in the streets, you may want to find a program that will provide support and help to relieve the stress you feel.

A group such as Big Brothers and Big Sisters may be able to help. Called a "mentor program," Big Brothers and Big Sisters give teenagers positive role models. In this program, adult volunteers take the place of a parent or friend. They are role models because many of them grew up under the same conditions as the teens in the group and are now successful. A teen has someone to talk to who will listen to problems and concerns and provide advice and support. Being involved in this program can help build self-esteem.

A teen may also gain new experiences through these groups. Teens can learn that there are more options in life than what they see—more beyond their own area, friends, and home. They can get away from peer pressure, gangs, drugs, and the isolation of their own neighborhood.

"I am not only graduating from high school this year, but I am going to college in the fall," says seventeen-year-old Aidan. "I've got to give a lot of credit to my Big

Brother, Steve. He's not really my big brother, but he comes from the Big Brothers organization.

"It's a long story, starting with my dad walking out on us a few years ago. He left me with my mom, three sisters, and my grandmother: all women! I couldn't stand it. I was always angry, ready to tear things apart. I wouldn't go to school, and I wouldn't do anything my mom or Gramma wanted me to. I was this close to joining a gang when I heard about Big Brothers. Before I met Steve, I was afraid he was going to be some goody-two-shoes, but no way. He grew up in my neighborhood, without a father, and now he owns a business.

"We would get together on Saturdays and do things, like shoot baskets. Steve always made me finish my homework first. Usually Gramma took my sisters with her to do the laundry, and my mother was working, so that the apartment was quiet. Steve convinced me to go to school and to stay in school. My teachers and the school counselor couldn't believe the change in me, but I think it's because Steve helped me to feel good about myself, and he helped me cope with a lot of stress. If he could succeed, then I could succeed."

You can relate one-on-one with a mentor, as Aidan did, to address your problems. You can also benefit from working with a group.

SUPPORT GROUPS

Support groups can help you cope with stress. In a support group, several people with similar problems get together with or without a counselor for discussion and support. Support groups cover a wide variety of subjects. You can find an appropriate support group whether you need to talk about your parents' divorce, your dad's unemployment, the illness or death (including suicide) of a family member or friend, an eating disorder, or a problem with drugs or alcohol.

In a support group you can share your feelings and anxieties with people who may feel the same way. When you learn that others are experiencing similar emotions, you know that you are not alone, and you know that you are not abnormal. It can boost your self-esteem and your ability to cope with your situation. People who belong to support groups are often less likely than others to respond negatively to stress.

A support group is a place where you can talk and learn how to handle your problems. It can help reduce stress by encouraging members to face their problems and find the courage to deal with them. Members can learn how others faced similar problems and succeeded in coping with them. Groups also provide social support and comfort among members, which is an important factor in reducing stress. You can share your successes as well as your stresses.

Participation in a support group can even improve physical health. Less stress means lower blood pressure and less muscle tension. People who experience the social support of a group tend to take better care of themselves by eating well, getting more sleep, exercising, and avoiding harmful habits such as smoking and drinking. These measures help to reduce the effects of stress, so it becomes a positive cycle.

A support group might be sponsored by a hospital, social service agency, church or synagogue, school, or just an interested group of friends or neighbors. If you find a need for a special support group in your community, try to organize it yourself. You are taking control of a situation and that, in itself, can help reduce stress.

A support group may be the only place where you can share your feelings about serious problems. Even a best friend may be uncomfortable talking to you. That's what happened to Alicia.

"Fiona and I grew up together, and we were always best friends," Alicia says. "When my dad died from cancer, Fiona seemed to disappear. After the funeral, she came with her parents to our house, but she just stood at the back of the room. When I went back to school, none of the kids seemed to want to talk to me. I felt so isolated. I was so stressed, I couldn't eat or sleep. All I wanted to do was sit on my bed and cry. My dad's death wasn't a big surprise, because he had been sick for a while; but I *was* surprised that my friends abandoned me.

"Luckily Mom signed me up for a bereavement support group at the Cancer Center. There I could talk to other kids who had lost a parent to cancer. I also learned how to manage my stress. It takes a long time to get over your grief, even with a support group. They don't give you a timetable and say you should be over your grief by a certain date. You feel comfortable, and that helps reduce the stress.

"It took a couple of months before the kids at school treated me normally again. Fiona told me she was afraid to talk to me because she didn't know what to say. She was afraid she would say the wrong thing and make me feel even worse. I've got to thank the support group for helping me not to feel totally alone."

A pastor or rabbi may lead a support group for those who have a family member who is terminally ill or dying. There are also special support groups for teens who have lost a family member to suicide. In this situation, the whole family will probably need counseling.

PEER COUNSELING

Recognizing that teens have the power to help other teens, many schools and religious organizations are establishing peer counseling groups. In peer counseling, young people are trained to steer other teens in the right direction.

By teaching problem-solving strategies and other skills, peer counseling gives teenagers the opportunity to solve many of their own conflicts. Peer counseling can be used to resolve conflicts between teens in school. Peer counselors can also help other teens to deal with personal problems.

Sixteen-year-old Glenn discovered his school's peer counseling group when he had some stressful problems at home. "I couldn't talk to my parents, because I thought they were the cause of all my problems in the first place," Glenn says. "I was ready to do something desperate, like running away. Then I started working with the peer counseling group. In a group like that, you can learn how other people handled similar problems. You also find out that you can cope, because they did. Your problem won't last forever if you deal with it in the right way. You need to talk, and you need someone to listen. At the same time, you listen to someone else, so you help each other."

Whatever the stressful situation in your life, there are resources you can turn to for help. These organizations are there for you to use when you need them. You will begin to realize that you can cope with your problems, even if it takes a long time before they no longer cause you stress. It is important for you to remember that you do not have to handle your problems alone. Feeling alone can be very stressful in itself.

CHAPTER 10

How *Not* to Cope
with Stress

"I'm sure that a lot of the teens who get into trouble with the law are really acting out as a way of coping with stress," says Ross, a social worker for a police department. "Today's teens have to put up with a lot of stress, a lot more than I ever did. There are problems at home, problems in school and out on the street, and worries about drugs and pregnancy. Even though they are educated about the risks of their behavior, kids still do things that get them into trouble. That's what frightens me. Kids are out stealing, setting fires, using drugs and alcohol. If their behavior is related to stress, then they are choosing coping mechanisms that are unhealthy."

When you are under stress, you want to cope with it in positive ways that reduce the stress. Often teens—and adults, too—deal with their stress in ways they think will reduce it, but these actions may actually increase stress.

124

You may try to mask your stress by rationalizing that it isn't so bad or that you don't need help; by denying that you are under stress; by acting out with violent, aggressive behavior; or by turning to drugs, alcohol or tobacco. These are the wrong actions to take. They can lead to more serious physical and emotional problems.

There are many activities that may seem to decrease stress for a brief period. Activities such as drinking beverages containing alcohol or caffeine, smoking, taking drugs, watching a lot of television, daydreaming, or simply ignoring the problem are "quick fix" solutions that do not solve anything. These actions not only do **not** reduce stress, but they are also likely to **increase** your stress. You must stop the cycle and find more productive ways to decrease the stress you feel.

A year ago, Kelly felt completely stressed out by all the homework she had to do. "Every time I turned something in, I got another assignment!" she said. "Papers take me a long time to write, and if I had a test during the same week that I had a paper due, forget it. There was no way I could get everything done. So I would 'wing it' on the test, and it really showed. I got so freaked out about writing papers that I would procrastinate and not start them until the night before. To 'relax,' I started watching tons of television—whatever was on, basically. While I sat on the couch and watched television, I ate whatever junk food was in the house. Of course, I didn't stop worrying about the paper. I worried more because I knew I was wasting time. Worrying more made me eat more. Once, I missed a paper deadline completely, and I didn't study at all for a big test. I had two lousy grades, my brain was fried from so much television, and I had gained fifteen pounds. For the first time, I really took a good look at what I was doing, and so did my mom! She made me go see the school counselor, who set up meetings with my teachers so we could talk about how to improve my study habits. I found out that there's a writing lab at my school to help kids write papers. I had no idea it existed. Now, I go there as soon as I get a paper assignment. My whole family is a lot more conscious of the amount of television we watch. The television is only on for an hour a night. I also talked with my doctor about nutrition, and I've noticed that eating right gives me more energy to do the things I need to do. Junk food doesn't even sound good anymore."

RATIONALIZING STRESS

Everyone experiences stress to some degree. Denying that you have stress, and therefore not dealing with it, is not a healthy response to your stress. First, you need to recognize that there is a problem. Then you can start to deal with the problem and start making changes. When you put off your problem, hoping it will just go away by itself, you are actually wasting the energy you need to respond to your stress in a positive way.

Because they want to avoid the stress a disaster might cause, some people may deny the possibility of a disaster, especially a natural disaster. They ignore warnings and do not even take simple precautions. However, preparing for a disaster or doing something to reduce the risk of disaster gives you a sense of control that can help to reduce stress.

ARTIFICIAL STRESS REDUCERS

Turning to alcohol, tobacco, or drugs is *not* the way to cope with stress. These substances may be popular remedies for stress, but they offer only temporary relief. Alcohol may make you feel relaxed and happy when you first try it. However, the more you drink, the less relaxed and happy you feel. Drinking can lead to a variety of physical and emotional problems, including liver and heart disease, anxiety, depression, and disturbed sleep.

Drugs and alcohol can be habit-forming. They create more problems and may only compound the stress you are feeling. When you are under the influence of drugs or alcohol you reduce your ability to control the sources of stress in your life. Control is an important factor in coping with stress.

In the short term, smoking may seem to reduce stress by making you feel more relaxed. Smoking may make you feel more alert and less anxious. In the long term, however, smoking causes a variety of physical problems which increase stress and the symptoms of stress, such as high blood pressure, heart disease, and breathing problems. Smoking may impair blood circulation and breathing, and can cause sleep disorders. It can also reduce your immunity to infectious diseases and may lead to stroke, heart disease, and cancer.

Prescribed medications and over-the-counter drugs, such as sleeping pills and tranquilizers, may help you to feel relaxed and can reduce the symptoms of stress. However, tranquilizers may make you drug dependent and can be very dangerous when taken in large doses or with alcohol or other drugs. They also can impair the way you feel and act during the day. They can make you feel tired or depressed.

The use of alcohol, tobacco, or drugs to cope with stress only covers up the symptoms of stress and does not deal with the source of stress. You need to go beyond just treating the symptoms to actually deal with the problem.

"I was so nervous about auditioning for the piano concerto competition, I was a real wreck," says sixteen-year-old Renata. "Everything seemed to hurt: my head, my stomach, my muscles. I was really stressed out. So, I took a tranquilizer pill that my doctor had prescribed. I also took some aspirin. It didn't work the way I had hoped. When I got to the audition, I was relaxed, but I also couldn't play very well. I couldn't concentrate on the music, and I kept making mistakes. Of course I didn't win the competition. As it turned out, the medication only made me feel depressed; and after it wore off, I had the biggest headache of my life."

THE EFFECTS OF FOOD AND DRINK

What you eat and drink—and the way you eat and drink—may seem to reduce stress, but poor eating and drinking habits can affect you emotionally as well as physically. For instance, caffeine—found in coffee and many colas—may at first create a feeling of alertness and better concentration, but these feelings are soon reduced, causing you to "crash" and feel sluggish later on. Too much caffeine can cause stomach disorders, irregular heartbeat, and headaches.

Candy and other foods containing sugar can give you a feeling of energy, but this is quickly followed by a letdown that leaves you feeling irritable and tired. Chocolate also contains caffeine. Sugary foods may also cause tooth decay and weight gain, two problems that can add to your stress. A balanced diet combined with exercise will keep your energy level steady and will help you maintain a healthy body weight.

EATING DISORDERS

Food is essential for living. For most people, eating can also be an enjoyable social event. However, there are people who turn to food—or turn away from food—to reduce their feelings of stress. Some may develop an eating disorder such as anorexia nervosa or bulimia. Others will overeat and gain a large amount of weight. Eating disorders are symptoms of stress. Improper eating habits will not reduce stress. They can only increase stress and may lead to serious health problems.

"I don't know what happened to my friend Alison," says Leah, sixteen. "Things seemed to be going so well for her. She was one of the best students in the class, she had the lead in the school play, she was even a homecoming princess for the big football game. But then she stopped eating and she started to lose a lot of weight. When I asked her what was wrong, the only thing she said was, 'It's hard for me to do everything that's expected of me.' Alison got so thin, she had to drop out of school at the end of her sophomore year and go into the hospital. Mom told me Alison had anorexia.

"Alison is back in school now, and she looks a little better. She told me that she has learned to manage her stress better. I didn't know that stress—or at least coping with stress in the wrong way—could affect you like that."

If you suspect that you or someone you know has an eating disorder, it is vital to seek medical help right away. Eating disorders can result in death if left untreated for too long.

PROBLEMS IN RELATIONSHIPS

Close relationships with family and friends are important. By giving you the opportunity to talk and to share feelings with people who care about you, these relationships can help you avoid stress as well as cope with stress. However, in an effort to deal with their stress, some teens find themselves involved in a harmful relationship. When your values differ greatly or your opinions conflict with a friend or relative, the relationship can be more stressful than helpful. Relationships that include physical or emotional abuse can only increase stress and may lead to serious physical or emotional damage.

"Acting Out"

Jane Gaitskill, a social worker who counsels teens, says that teens often react to stress by acting out, being difficult, and getting into trouble at home or school. They may refuse to do their homework and may turn to drugs. "This behavior will never reduce stress, and probably will increase it," Gaitskill says.

Venting your anger may sometimes make you feel better, but it is not the proper way to deal with your stress. When you curse, threaten, intimidate, or try to exert excessive control by demanding your way and being the center of attention, you are not taking action to reduce your stress.

VIOLENT AND RECKLESS BEHAVIOR

Violent behavior is always unacceptable. If your stress makes you feel like lashing out, turn instead to physical exercise or work. David lifts weights when he feels angry.

"All that energy I might waste on anger goes into my lifts and helps to improve them," he says.

"I like my after-school ceramics class for that reason," says Glenda, fourteen. "When I get angry, I feel like throwing things. In ceramics class, I can really throw that clay on the wheel and pound it. Instead of breaking things, I come out with something creative."

When a teen has survived a disaster, but is not coping well in the aftermath, he or she might adopt the attitude that "nothing can hurt me now." He or she may turn to inappropriate behavior and try risky activities, such as drugs or reckless driving.

Expressing anger by acting out violently cannot reduce stress. On the other hand, holding in feelings can lead to serious physical and emotional stress symptoms. That is why it is important to communicate your feelings in an appropriate manner. Both burying feelings and acting out are the wrong ways to cope.

NEGATIVE THINKING

You are thinking negatively when you dwell on the bad side of an issue, exaggerating the negative and minimizing the positive. Negative thinking will not reduce your stress, but can only add to it. Negative thoughts can lead to inappropriate feelings which in turn lead to unacceptable behavior.

Negative thinking may include the following:

- **Worrying about stressful situations** without taking some action to solve them. Some people even worry about situations that don't yet exist.
- **Deciding that you have to solve your prob-**

lems by yourself: "No one else can help me with this problem."

- **Trying to handle all your problems at once:** If you believe that you must deal with—and eliminate—all your problems at once, rather than working on one problem at a time over a long period of time, you may not succeed in eliminating any problem.
- **Overgeneralizing:** "I'm always wrong," "Nobody likes me," "If I can't solve this problem, I can't solve any problems."
- **Jumping to conclusions:** "I know they won't like my speech in English class."

Many of these negative thoughts can become self-fulfilling prophesies, meaning that thinking about them will make them come true. You may not prepare your speech well enough because "nobody will like it anyway." Fearing rejection at a party or when starting a new school, you may not try to be friendly to others, and they *will* reject you because they think you are unfriendly.

Negative thinking occurs when you worry not only about a situation, but also about the stress the situation will cause you. That worry can be even more stressful than the situation itself.

This happened to fifteen-year-old Mia. She arranged a trip to the theater for her church's youth group. She sent out publicity, took reservations, bought the tickets, and arranged for transportation. At the same time, Mia worried whether her friends would like the play.

"I was under too much stress," Mia says. "Here I was doing all this work, which was stressful to begin with. Instead of giving myself credit for doing a good job, I worried whether people would like the play, which only added to my stress. It was giving me headaches and stomachaches. In fact, on the night of the play, I had a hard time enjoying the show. I think if I had emphasized the positive instead of the negative, I would have had a lot less stress, and I would have enjoyed the evening a lot more. After all my worrying, everyone loved the play, and a lot of people thanked me for making the arrangements. I wished I could have been more confident from the beginning."

Think about how you usually respond to stressful situations. If you react with negative thinking or denial, or if you react by getting angry, resorting to violence, taking drugs, smoking, drinking, or eating badly, you are adding stress, not reducing it. Social worker Jim Gorski advises teens to act upon their stress, not just react to it. Do something positive to bring about a change which will reduce or eliminate the stressor, or make a change in your response to that stressor.

CHAPTER 11

Avoiding Stress (Sometimes)

"I think writing this term paper has been a real education, and not just because I learned a lot about the subject of the paper," says sixteen-year-old Rashid. "I was really stressed out over this paper. I started it too late, and I had to rush at the end. I skipped meals to work on it, and I couldn't sleep at night worrying about it. That only made it harder to write the paper the next day. It gave me a giant-sized headache.

"I finished the paper and handed it in on time. But I've learned my lesson. Now I know that I could have avoided a lot of stress if I had started earlier and was more organized. I should have eaten right and gotten more sleep, and even done some exercising and relaxing. That would have done it: good-bye stress!"

STRESS IS PART OF LIFE

Everyone experiences stress from time to time to some degree. It's not possible to avoid all stressful situations.

You would not want to avoid all stress, anyway. In some instances, a little stress is good; it may help you perform better on the basketball court, or push you to study longer for an exam. We will discuss the positive side of stress later in this chapter.

There are things you can do to avoid some stress, such as establishing good eating and sleeping patterns, getting organized and planning ahead, and communicating with family and friends.

There are many good reasons to make wise lifestyle choices. Eating right, getting enough sleep, and exercising (all those things your parents, teachers, and doctors tell you to do) will help keep you physically healthy. These are also just the kinds of things that can help you to avoid stress, reduce stress, and cope with stress. If you are in good physical shape when you experience stress, your stress may have less of a negative effect on your body.

Establish good eating habits. Good eating habits include having a good breakfast every day. A good meal to start the day raises your energy level, so you are better prepared to face the stressors that may await you. During the day, eat regular meals that include fruits, vegetables, protein, and whole grains. Cut down on fats, salt, and sugar.

Avoid caffeine and alcohol. Eating or drinking products with caffeine—including chocolate, cola, and coffee—can make you feel stressed even when there is no reason for the stress. Caffeine can interfere with a restful sleep. Alcohol is a depressant, which means that, even if at first it makes you feel better, it will eventually impair your ability to cope with stress.

Get enough sleep. When you are overtired, a problem may seem to be much bigger than it actually is. Try to maintain a regular sleep schedule, and get up at about the same time every day, even on weekends. This kind of routine is less stressful than not getting enough sleep during the week and then trying to catch up on the weekends.

Learn relaxation techniques. To reduce stress, use relaxation techniques, such as deep breathing, especially before a stressful event like giving a speech or taking a test. Regular **exercise** not only makes you feel better and look better, but it can also modify the way your body responds to stress. Your body can recover more quickly from the physical effects of stress if it is in good physical condition.

Learn problem-solving techniques. When you are under stress—or, before a situation causes you stress—take time to understand the real problem and the best way to approach it. Consider more than one option.

Get organized. If you organize your activities and manage your time effectively, you will not only avoid a lot of stress, but you will also discover many other benefits. You are probably a busy person with many activities, including classes, homework, sports, music lessons, or other after-school activities, such as a part-time job. You may have a variety of responsibilities at home, including babysitting, cleaning, and helping out with meals. When you have many activities, you can become overwhelmed, which can cause stress. If you try to do everything at once, you may actually accomplish very little, and that can cause even more stress.

It's a good idea to keep a calendar, not only to write down school assignments, but for other dates and appointments, too. Leila has two calendars, one just for her social life, the other one for school. "I can't live without either one," Leila says. "The first things I buy when school starts are my assignment notebooks."

Set priorities. Instead of trying to do all your activities in too little time, pace yourself and do one task at a time. List your activities in order of importance and do the most important ones first. If you have a task that can be completed quickly, you might do that one first to give yourself a morale boost. If one task is overwhelming by itself, try to break it up into parts; for instance, you may not be able to wash all the windows in your apartment in one day, but you may be able to wash all the front windows and get the back ones done in a day or two.

If you need assistance with a difficult project, don't hesitate to **ask for help**. You will not only find your work easier, which helps reduce stress, but you will enjoy the support of another person.

Leave some unscheduled time in your work for interruptions or emergencies, as well as time for relaxation or exercise; remember, they are stress fighters. Don't forget to **mix in some fun** activities with your more serious obligations.

It's stressful when you don't have enough time to accomplish what you need to do and what you want to do. Good **time management** can help to prevent that stress. First, **set goals**. Make a list of things you have to do and things you want to do. Be realistic. Include short-term goals for the next few days and weeks. Don't forget to plan for long-term goals as well. For instance, if one of your goals is making the varsity track team, you have to include in your time schedule the practice and training it will take to reach that goal.

Keep everything in perspective. When setting goals, be realistic. Goals should be neither too high, so they are unreachable; nor too low, so they offer no incentive. Accept that you can't do everything. **Have a sense of humor and optimism**.

Try to **maintain a balance** between extremes in your life. Find the "happy medium" between trying to accomplish everything by yourself and only depending on the support and assistance of others. Maintain a balance between what you ought to do and what you want to do. Be aware of what you can control and know that you can't have control over every situation.

Get involved in activities at school; in your church, synagogue, or mosque; or in the community. Volunteer work can boost your feelings of self-esteem.

If you work part-time or full-time, try to **do something that you enjoy** so you care enough to do a good job. If you don't care for the work, try at least to pick one part of it that you do like. If you get no satisfaction at all from your work, you will only add to your stress.

"I guess I'm lucky I got this job as a receptionist for a manufacturer," says April, seventeen. "The pay is pretty good, but the work is sort of boring. I actually started to feel nervous because I wasn't doing *enough* work. But then I noticed that the display case in the reception area was just sitting there empty. I asked my boss if I could put in some kind of display, and he said okay.

"Planning what to put in the display case uses my creativity. Working on it fills in the time when I don't have anything else to do. Now work is much more interesting for me, and I look forward to coming to work. I don't have those stressful feelings anymore, either."

Stay in control of yourself and your life as much as possible. Not all stressors can be avoided. Others are completely under your control. For instance, an unplanned pregnancy can be a major source of stress, but it can be prevented. Become informed about pregnancy, birth control, and sexually transmitted diseases, and act positively from that knowledge.

For the stressors that can't be avoided, a **positive atti-tude** can make a difference in how much stress you feel. For example, change can be stressful, but viewing change as a challenge or a new experience can reduce the stress. Try to be open to new experiences.

When you are in control of a situation, it gives you the confidence that you can manage the situation and even turn events to your advantage; you then feel less stressed. The less control you have over a situation, the more stress-ful it is.

Scott, sixteen, knows all about control and stress. "I work after school for an auto mechanic, Tom. So does Jake, another guy I know from high school. When I work on my own, there's a lot of pressure to do a good job and to get it done on time. I really like doing this work, so I don't feel stressed. I've gotten a lot of compliments and some good tips, too.

"When I have to work with Jake, I start to feel stressed, because the quality of the job is no longer in my control," Scott continues. "A few weeks ago, Jake messed up on a good customer's car. Tom yelled at Jake, but he also yelled at me for not catching the mistake. When I got home I really felt sick. I don't want to quit, but I can't take the stress I get when I'm not in control of a situation. I'm going to have to start paying a lot more attention to Jake's work, and I'm going to talk to Tom about giving Jake some better training." Scott's commitment to do a good job and his striving for control will actually help him to avoid stress.

Control also means you need to **think for yourself** and not give in to peer pressure. Samuel Huff, a counselor in a midwestern inner city school, advises his students to be independent. "Don't just go along with the crowd. Think for yourself; use your own good mind. You know right from wrong; so don't go along when you know something is wrong," Huff says. This is a sign of emotional and moral maturity.

As you mature, you need to **take responsibility for your actions**. Taking responsibility puts you in control, and control helps you avoid or reduce stress. To make it easier, try role playing. You can rehearse what you want to say and how you want to act in order to resist peer pressure to smoke, drink, or take drugs. A lot of people— adults and other teens—may be ready to tell you what you should do. However, this is your opportunity to think for yourself and take control.

Don't fear stress, but do anticipate it. If you **anticipate stress**, you may be able to avoid it or reduce it. However, there are two sides to anticipating stress. On the positive side, when you feel that a situation may cause you stress, you can take time out, assess the situation, and decide on a response. "Rehearse" stressful situations. This way you can gain some sense of control. You may not be able to control every situation, but you can plan your response and reduce the stress that an event may cause. The negative side of anticipation occurs when you only worry that a situation will cause you stress. That worry can be even more stressful than the circumstance itself.

To calm down when anticipating stress, ask yourself: "What is the worst thing that can happen?" Then consider how likely it is that the worst will occur. Plan in advance what you will do if it *does* happen. This will help you feel more prepared for any outcome.

Being independent and in control does not mean that you should avoid contact with other people. On the contrary, many social workers and psychologists agree that having **close relationships** with family, friends, and other people in the community is one of the best ways to avoid stress or to cope with stress. Seek out at least one adult whom you trust and who cares about you, such as a parent, an aunt or uncle, a teacher, counselor, coach, member of the clergy, neighbor, or employer. Close relationships with relatives and friends help you to avoid some stress and to reduce the symptoms of stress. However, it is important that you belong to a peer group that shares your values.

THE GOOD SIDE OF STRESS

Everyone experiences stress to some degree in their everyday lives. Stress cannot be totally eliminated from your life. You probably wouldn't want to avoid all stress, anyway. That would mean that your life was pretty dull. Remember, some stress comes from happy events, such as graduating or going on vacation. A moderate amount of stress can give us increased energy and motivation to succeed. Beyond keeping life interesting and exciting, stress has several other benefits.

Stress can be a warning sign of other problems in our lives. It tells us that something needs to be recognized and acted upon. You can learn from stress. "I started getting tight muscles whenever I went to gymnastics practice. I couldn't perform at my best; it was almost like an injury," says Janie, fifteen. "My coach said it was stress, probably because I had so many other activities. I was trying to get top grades in school, too. My 'injury' made me look at my life. I needed to get organized, and I needed to decide if I really should be doing all the activities I was involved in.

"Well, I did get organized, and I did drop a couple of activities that I was only doing because someone else thought I should do them. Now I don't have the tight muscles, and I'm performing better in gymnastics. I even have more time for studying. I guess you could say that stress helped me because it forced me to make changes that improved my life."

When you rehearse or prepare for a potential situation that may be stressful, such as a natural disaster, you are also educating yourself. Learning about disaster preparedness may not only reduce the stress you feel before and after the disaster occurs, but may also provide knowledge that will help you cope with day-to-day problems. The fight-or-flight reaction that takes over after a disaster can help you to help yourself and others.

Preparing for a disaster or doing something to reduce the risk of disaster gives you some control over the situation and can help reduce stress. When you do survive a disaster, you gain new feelings of confidence and self-esteem; you have mastered a tremendous challenge.

A moderate amount of stress can help improve athletic performance. You need some stress or stimulation to do your best. A little stress can be useful, increasing your performance and efficiency. However, a lot of stress or continuous stress can lead to a bad performance.

Change can be stressful, but it can also be viewed as an opportunity. Change may help you improve the quality of your life by giving you new choices. When you deal with stress, you have an opportunity to re-evaluate your life, to set new goals and priorities, and to improve relationships. Stress can be beneficial, but only in a moderate amount, and only when you try to cope with it. You cannot eliminate all stress, but you can deal with it in many ways and that is how you can improve your life.

You can look at stress and your efforts to cope with stress as a challenge and an opportunity. Successfully coping with stress can improve your self-esteem and competence. When you deal with your stress, you grow as a person. By using problem-solving skills and finding alternatives to stressful situations, you may find your life going in a new direction.

Glossary

anorexia nervosa An eating disorder characterized by a dramatic weight loss, compulsive dieting, lack of appetite, and fear of gaining weight.

anti-Semitic Showing prejudice against people of Jewish descent.

biofeedback A technique for monitoring and modifying the body's response to stress.

bulimia An eating disorder in which eating binges are followed by strict dieting, strenuous exercise, vomiting and/or the use of laxatives in order to purge food.

compulsive disorder A psychological condition in which a person performs certain actions repeatedly for no apparent reason.

crisis A situation of extreme change, with either a positive or negative impact.

fight-or-flight response The natural human impulse to defend oneself or flee when confronted with a threatening situation.

immunity The body's ability to fight off or protect against disease.

insomnia Difficulty or inability to fall asleep or sleep soundly.

phobia A strong fear, usually irrational and excessive, of a particular thing or situation.

positive thinking A confident, self-assured way of looking at oneself and the world.

post-traumatic stress disorder An extreme stress response arising from a disaster or crisis in which a person relives the trauma and continues to be emotionally tied up in it.

144

prejudice   The expression of bias or intolerance against another person without reason.

racism   The belief that a race of people is superior to others.

Restricted Environment Stimulus Therapy (R.E.S.T.)   A method of reducing stress by minimizing all external stimuli.

sexually transmitted disease   Any disease that is transmitted from person to person through sexual contact.

stress   Mental or physical tension as a response to a condition, situation, or incident.

stressor   A condition, situation, or incident that causes stress.

Type A personality   A person who is usually tense, aggressive, and driven to perform or succeed.

Appendix

RESOURCES

Listed below are a few of the many organizations that can help you with your stress or with a specific source of stress. You can also find information at your local public library, community center, mental health association, or hospital. Your local telephone directory also lists organizations and resources for help in your area.

In the United States:

Alateen
P.O. Box 862
Midtown Station
New York, NY 10018
(212) 302-7240

American Red Cross/Disaster Mental Health Program
Mid-America Chapter
43 East Ohio Street
Chicago, IL 60611
(312) 440-2140

American Self-Help Clearing House
St. Clares-Riverside Medical Center
25 Pocono Road
Denville, NJ 07834
(800) 367-6274
(201) 625-7101
e-mail: ashc@bc.cybernex.net(american)
Web site: http://www.cmhc.com/selfhelp

Big Brothers Big Sisters of America
230 North 13th Street
Philadelphia, PA 19107
(215) 567-7000
e-mail: bbbsa@aol.com
Web site: http://www.bbbsa.org

Families Anonymous
P.O. Box 3475
Culver City, CA 90231-3475
(800) 736-9805
(310) 313-5800
e-mail: famanon@aol.com

Families with Children
Hospice of the North Shore
2821 Central Street
Evanston, IL 60201
(847) HOSPICE (467-7423)

National Association of Anorexia Nervosa
  and Associated Disorders
Box 7
Highland Park, IL 60035
(847) 831-3438

National Institute of Mental Health
U.S. Department of Health and Human Services
5600 Fishers Lane
Rockville, MD 20857
(301) 443-4513
for information on Depression: (800) 421-4211
for information on Panic: (800) 64-PANIC (647-2642)
for information on Anxiety: (888) ANXIETY (269-4389)
e-mail: nimhinfo@nih.gov
Web site: http://www.nimh.nih.gov

National Mental Health Association Information Center
(800) 969-NMHA (6642)

Overeaters Anonymous
6075 Zenith Court NE
Rio Rancho, NM 87124
(505) 891-2664

Planned Parenthood Federation of America
810 Seventh Avenue
New York, NY 10019
(212) 541-7800
e-mail: communications@ppfa.org
Web site: http://www.ppfa.org/ppfa

Self Help Center
150 North Wacker Drive
Chicago, IL 60606
(312) 368-9070

In Canada:
A1-Anon/Alateen
101 A Newkirk Road South
Richmond Hill, Ontario L4C 2C6
(416) 366-4072

Canadian Mental Health Association
2160 Yonge Street
Toronto, Ontario M4S 2Z3
(416) 484-7750

Planned Parenthood Federation of Canada
1 Nicholas Street, Suite 430
Ottawa, Ontario K1N 7B7
(613) 241-4474

For Further Reading

Buckingham, Robert, Ph.D., and Huggard, Sandra. *Coping with Grief*, rev. ed. New York: Rosen Publishing Group, 1993.

Feldman, Robert S. *Understanding Stress*. New York: Franklin Watts, 1992.

Inlander, Charles B. *Stress: Ways to Relieve Tension and Stay Healthy*. New York: Walker & Co., 1996.

Krementz, Jill. *How It Feels When a Parent Dies*. New York: Alfred A. Knopf, 1988.

———. *How It Feels When Parents Divorce*. New York: Alfred A. Knopf, 1984.

Managing Stress from Morning to Night. Alexandria, VA: Time-Life Books, 1987.

Mason, L. John, Ph.D. *Stress Passages: Surviving Life's Transitions Gracefully*. Berkeley, CA: Celestial Arts, 1988.

Packard, Gwen K. *Coping When a Parent Goes Back to Work*. New York: Rosen Publishing Group, 1995.

Simpson, Carolyn. *Coping with an Unplanned Pregnancy*, rev. ed. New York: Rosen Publishing Group, 1994.

Wilson, Miriam J. *Stress Stoppers for Children and Adolescents*. Shepherdstown, WV: Rocky River Publishers, 1988.

Index

A

abortion, 52

abuse (emotional, sexual, and verbal), 23, 42, 119, 130

accidents/injuries, 9, 37, 52, 54–56, 61, 63, 81, 103, 105

AIDS, 5, 45–46, 49, 53, 117

alcohol and drinking, 5, 9, 10, 18, 23, 24, 26, 35, 37, 45, 47, 68, 112, 113, 116, 121, 124, 125, 126–127, 133, 135, 140

anger, 4, 5, 6, 9, 10, 23, 25, 43, 53, 54, 58, 60, 62, 64, 71, 73, 83, 99, 102, 110, 111, 130–131, 133

anxiety, 5, 9, 10, 11, 36, 40, 59, 64, 65, 88, 112, 127

B

Big Brothers and Big Sisters, 119–120

biofeedback, 88, 89–90

breathe properly, 87–88, 136

C

caffeine and sugar, 18, 26, 84, 125, 128, 135

carelessness, 10, 11, 12

change, 17, 34, 49, 50, 52, 53, 59, 96, 142

communication, 98–100, 102, 111, 131, 135

concentrate, inability to, 9, 11

counselors and therapists, 31, 36, 39, 55–56, 59, 63, 68, 70, 73, 74, 82, 93, 95, 97, 109–123, 125–126, 141

crime, 36, 39–41, 42, 46, 47–48, 50, 53. 67, 116–117, 124

crises, 51–68, 84, 111, 113, 114–115

crying, 9, 32, 56, 73, 103, 122

D

dating, 5, 44–46, 47

death, 10–11, 18, 21, 23, 37, 40, 42, 52, 53–56, 61, 63, 67, 75, 77, 103–105, 111, 113, 119, 121, 122

depression, 4, 5, 6, 9, 10, 11, 31, 32, 36, 40, 42, 43, 53, 54, 57, 58, 63, 71, 72, 112, 127, 128, 135

disasters, 7, 11, 18, 40, 51–68, 84, 95, 107, 108, 111, 114–115, 116, 126, 131, 142

discussing feelings, 5–6, 27, 54, 58, 60, 62, 68, 70, 82, 94–108, 115